"ILLUSTRATED BOOK OF MARY"

Edited by:
Fr. Michael Sullivan
Archdiocese of New York

Marian History Devotions
Julie Cragon
Nashville, TN

William J. Hirten Co.
96 Frank Mossberg Drive Attleboro, MA.

Illustrated Book of Mary

INTRODUCTION

The Blessed Virgin Mary plays a key role in the beliefs of many Christians. Church theologians carefully distinguish between the type of worship due to God, latria, and the veneration given to the saints, dulia. Catholic theology includes a type of veneration, hyperdulia, paid specifically to the Mother of God, the Blessed Virgin Mary, because it is pleasing to God that we honor His Mother. Her many different titles have developed from her personal life, her places of honor in the life of the Church, her role in the plan of our salvation and her intercession to God on our behalf. Devotion to her has not just come about because of the writings of the saints and the Church Fathers, but also due to the belief in Marian apparitions and the reports of miracles and healings. Because of her special role in union with God, when we honor Mary, when we pray the rosary and the stations and the many other prayers associated with her, we honor God.

Our Lady of Grace

I turn to thee, O Mother dear,
In humble supplication,
Asking that I follow thee
You are my inspiration.
I ask for very simple things,
To walk in lowly ways,
But may I always walk with thee
The remainder of my days?
Give me the grace I see in Thee,
And make me be forgiving,
Let me ne'er abandon Him,
In prayer and thanksgiving.
I leave with thee and with thy Son
These fervent prayers of mine.
Knowing that from Him through you
Comes every gift divine.

Our Lady of Grace
HISTORY AND DEVOTION

Our Lady of Grace is one of the most popular titles given to Mary. In the Gospel of Luke, the angel Gabriel greets Mary as "highly favored one". The Greek word used in this greeting is kecharitomene which translates "completely graced".

The Latin word used is gratia plena which translates "full of grace". Mary's role as Mother of Jesus, the Source of our Grace, gives her the privilege of being the vessel through which that same grace reaches humanity. St. Bernard says, "God could have dispensed His graces according to His good pleasure, without making use of this aqueduct (Mary), but it was His wish to provide this means whereby grace would reach you."

Pope Benedict XVI says, "Our Lady is like a celestial stream through which the flow of all graces and gifts reaches the soul of all wretched mortals." As Our Lady appeared to St. Catherine Laboure in France in 1830, brilliant rays shown from the jeweled rings on her fingers. Our Lady said, "These rays symbolize the graces I shed upon those who ask for them. The gems from which rays do not fall are the graces for which souls forget to ask."

She asked Catherine to have a medal struck of the vision and told her that graces would be bestowed abundantly to all who wore the medal with confidence.

During other appearances of Our Lady, she promises graces for those who pray the rosary, who attend Mass and who go frequently to confession. As our Mother, Our Lady wants us to receive all the graces that we need to obtain Heaven.

She is our Mediator who passes graces through her hands. As we pray, "Hail Mary, Full of Grace," she hears and answers our call.

Feast Day: 31 May
Name Meaning: Full of Grace
Patron Saint of: Universal

Immaculate Conception

*O Immaculate Virgin! Mary, conceived without
sin! Remember, you were miraculously preserved
from even the shadow of sin, because you were
destined to become not only the Mother of God,
but also the mother, the refuge, and the advocate
of man; penetrated therefore, with the most lively
confidence in your never failing intercession,
we most humbly implore you to look with favor
upon the intentions of his novena, and to obtain
for us the graces and the favors we request.
You know, O Mary, how often our hearts are the
sanctuaries of God, who abhors iniquity.
Obtain for us, then, that angelic purity which was
your favorite virtue, that purity of heart which
will attach us to God alone,
and that purity of intention
which will consecrate every thought, word, and
action to His greater glory. Obtain also for us a
constant spirit of prayer and self denial, that we
may recover by penance that innocence which
we have lost by sin, and at length attain safely to
that blessed abode of the saints,
where nothing defiled can enter.
O Mary, conceived without sin, pray for us who
have recourse to thee.*

Immaculate Conception
HISTORY AND DEVOTION

Immaculate Conception is the title given to Mary that celebrates her conception free from original sin. Pope Pius IX proclaimed the Immaculate Conception a dogma of the Church on December 8, 1854.

"The Most Blessed Virgin Mary was, from the first moment of her conception, by a singular grace and privilege of Almighty God, and by virtue of the merits of Jesus Christ, Savior of the human race, preserved immune from all stain of original sin". He sited Genesis 3:15 where God told the serpent, "I will put enmity between you and the woman, between your seed and her seed".

The Church understands this to mean that this woman would never be under the power of sin. Mary would forever be in that exalted state of grace which the serpent had destroyed in man.

Her continual union with grace explains her enmity with the serpent. Therefore, the Church believes that Mary was not only conceived without sin but was also free of sin throughout her life.

In Luke 1:28, theologians believed that the angel Gabriel's greeting which translates, "Hail, full of grace", meant that Mary was fully favored and filled with an abundance of grace.

God's grace kept her free from sin throughout her life. God chose her from the beginning to be the Mother of Jesus and thus, made her worthy and without sin.

In 1858, in Lourdes, France, the Blessed Virgin Mary appeared to Bernadette Soubirous eighteen times. During one of the apparitions, Our Lady told Bernadette to tell the priests to have a chapel built and processions held there.

The priest told Bernadette to ask the lady her name. Mary responded, "I am the Immaculate Conception".

Feast Day: December 8
Patron Saint of: United States

Our Lady of Lourdes

O ever Immaculate Virgin,
Mother of mercy,
Health of the sick, Refuge of sinners,
Comforter of the afflicted, you know my
wants, my troubles, and my sufferings.
Cast upon me a look of mercy.
By appearing in the Grotto of Lourdes,
you were pleased to make it
a privileged sanctuary,
where you dispense your favors;
and where many sufferers have
obtained the cure of their infirmities,
both spiritual and corporal.
I come, therefore, with the most
unbounded confidence to implore
your maternal intercession.
Obtain, O loving Mother,
the granting of my requests.
Through gratitude for favors, I will
endeavor to imitate your virtues that
I may one day share your glory.
Amen.

Our Lady of Lourdes
HISTORY AND DEVOTION

Our Lady of Lourdes is the title given to the Blessed Virgin Mary when she appeared in Lourdes, France.

On February 11, 1858, Bernadette Soubirous went to gather firewood with her sister and a friend in the foothills of the Pyrenees in southern France. Bernadette was weak from her asthma and fell behind the other girls.

Near the river, she heard a rushing sound in the grotto at the bottom of the mountain.

She turned to see a bright light, and within the light, a beautiful lady dressed in white.

As she approached, she saw that the lady had yellow roses at her feet and was holding a rosary.

After Bernadette knelt and prayed the rosary, the lady disappeared. Three days later, the lady appeared again in the grotto but only Bernadette could see her. The lady asked Bernadette to continue to come to the grotto and as she did, more and more people followed her.

On February 25, the lady told Bernadette to dig in the dirt and drink the water that would come from her digging.

With hundreds of people watching, she drank the muddy water.

By the next day, the water was flowing from the place where she had dug, and on March 1, a woman was cured of paralysis after dipping her hand in the spring. The lady then told Bernadette to tell the priests to have a chapel built and processions held there. The priest told Bernadette to ask the lady her name.

When Bernadette returned and told him that she was the Immaculate Conception, the priest knew that the apparitions were real because Bernadette would have never heard those words. The Blessed Mother appeared to Bernadette a total of eighteen times and a large Basilica was built near the grotto.

The Church has recognized 67 known cures in the waters at Lourdes which still flow endlessly for the millions of pilgrims that visit each year.

Feast Day: February 11
Name Meaning: town in France
Patron Saint of: France

Our Lady of Fatima

I come from Heaven,
I am the Lady of the Rosary.
I have come to warn the faithful
to amend their lives
and to ask pardon for their sins.
They must not offend Our Lord any more,
for He is already too grievously offended
by the sins of men.
People must say the Rosary.
If people do as I ask,
many souls will be converted
and there will be peace.

Our Lady of Fatima
History and Devotion

Our Lady of Fatima is the title given to the Blessed Virgin Mary when she appeared at Fatima, Portugal, between May and October of 1917, to three shepherd children.

Lucia Santos and her cousins Jacinta and Francisco Marto were tending sheep when a flash of bright light caught their attention and settled above a tree. Within the light was a Lady dressed in white with a rosary in her hand who said she was from Heaven. She asked the children to meet her at the same spot on the thirteenth of the next five consecutive months and to pray the rosary daily for world peace.

On June 13, Mary told them that Francisco and Jacinta would go to heaven soon and Lucia would remain to promote devotion to her Immaculate Heart. She added a prayer after each decade of the rosary. On July 13, about five thousand people gathered, but only the children could see as Mary spread out her hands and gave them a vision of hell. She predicted another war and asked for the consecration of Russia to her Immaculate Heart.

She gave the children three secrets and asked that people receive Communion of reparation on the first Saturday of each month. A government official jailed the children on August 13, threatening to boil them in oil if they did not tell him the secrets, but they would have died for their faith. On August 19, Mary appeared to them in a different place. During the apparition on September 13, over thirty thousand people witnessed a shower of white petals.

On October 13, after a heavy rain, seventy thousand people witnessed what was called the miracle of the sun.

The children saw Our Lady and St. Joseph with the Child Jesus blessing the world, Jesus blessing the crowd and Mary as Our Lady of Sorrows and Our Lady of Mount Carmel. Lucia continued to receive visions of Our Lady and in 1927 revealed the first two secrets.

In 1989, Lucia announced the acceptance of the consecration of Russia to the Immaculate Heart by Pope John Paul II; the same year that the Berlin Wall fell. In 2000, Pope John Paul II revealed the third secret interpreting it as a prediction of his assassination attempt. Lucia died in 2005.

Feast Day: May 13
Patron Saint of: Portugal

Our Lady of Guadalupe

O our Lady of Guadalupe,
mystical rose, make intercession
for Holy Church,
protect the Sovereign Pontiff,
help all those who invoke you
in their necessities, and since you
are the ever Virgin Mary
and Mother of the true God,
obtain for us from your most holy
Son the grace of keeping our faith,
sweet hope in the midst
of bitterness of life,
burning charity and the precious
gift of final perseverance.
500 days indulgence

Our Lady of Guadalupe
HISTORY AND DEVOTION

Our Lady of Guadalupe is the name given to the Blessed Virgin Mary when she appeared in Mexico. On December 9, 1531, Juan Diego was on his way to Mass in Mexico City when he heard a woman's voice calling him as he reached the hill at Tepeyac. Climbing the hill, he encountered the woman who identified herself as the Virgin Mary.

She instructed Juan Diego to go to the bishop of Mexico and take her request that he build a sanctuary so that she could make known to all her devoted children her love, her compassion and her protection. The bishop would not listen to Juan Diego. The next day, Mary appeared again and repeated her request. This time, the bishop told Juan Diego to bring him proof of the apparition.

But the next day, Juan's uncle was seriously sick and Juan went to get a priest to give the last rites. He tried to hurry past the hill but Our Lady met him and promised that his uncle was already cured. She asked Juan to climb the hill and gather flowers for her. Despite the cold of mid-December, Juan found a variety of Castilian roses and gathered them into his tilma, or cloak. He brought them to Mary who arranged them in his cloak and sent him off to show them to the bishop. When Juan was finally allowed to see the bishop, he opened his cloak and the roses fell to the floor. He was surprised to see the bishop kneeling before him looking at the full size image of Mary imprinted on his cloak. Her image was just as Juan Diego had described her. Juan Diego returned home to find his uncle, whom Mary had also visited, completely cured. In his own language, his uncle told those present that she called herself what sounded like Guadalupe, which was a famous Marian Shrine in Spain. The bishop ordered a church to be built as Mary had requested and the cloak with the image was enshrined there. A basilica was built in 1976 in Mexico City and Juan Diego's tilma with the image of Our Lady was moved to the Basilica.

Feast Day: December 12
Name Meaning: town in Mexico
Patron Saint of: pro-life, Americas

Our Lady of the Miraculous Medal

Virgin Mother of God,
Mary Immaculate,
I unite myself to you
under your title of Our Lady
of the Miraculous Medal.
May this medal be for me
a sure sign of your motherly
affection for me
and a constant reminder
of my duties toward you.
While wearing it,
may I be blessed by your
loving protection
and preserved in the grace
of your Son.
Most powerful Virgin,
Mother of our Savior,
keep me close to you every
moment of my life,
so that like you I may live
and act according
to the example of your Son.
Amen.

Our Lady of the Miraculous Medal

History and Devotion

Our Lady of the Miraculous Medal is the title given to the Blessed Virgin Mary when she appeared to a Sister of Charity of St. Vincent de Paul in Paris.

On July 18, 1830, Sr. Catherine Laboure was awakened by a young child standing at the end of her bed, calling for her to come, "The Blessed Virgin is waiting for you". Sister Catherine followed the boy to the Chapel where she knelt at the altar rail and waited. She heard the rustling of material before she saw the Blessed Mother come and sit in the priest's chair. Sister Catherine ran to her, and resting her hands on the knees of Mary listened for hours as she was instructed about how to act in times of trials she would encounter.

She predicted the terrible Revolution of 1830 in France and the Franco-Prussian War of 1860.

She told Sr. Catherine of a special mission that God had for her and the contradictions she would face. She asked Sr. Catherine to tell no one of her visit except her confessor Father Aladel.

On November 27, 1830 while in the chapel in meditation with other sisters, Sister Catherine again heard the rustling of material and the

Blessed Virgin appeared, standing on a globe and holding a smaller globe on top of a cross she seemed to offer to God.

When the globe disappeared, Mary lifted her hands that were covered with jewels. From some of the jewels, rays of light shown which she said were symbols of the graces that would be given to all who asked for them.

The jewels that had no rays were symbols of unclaimed graces. An oval frame outlined the figure bearing in gold letters the words "O Mary, conceived without sin, pray for us who have recourse to thee". When the frame revolved, on the back the letter M was surmounted by a cross with a crossbar underneath, and beneath that the Sacred Heart of Jesus surrounded by a crown of thorns and the Sacred Heart of Mary pierced by a sword. She asked Catherine to have a medal made after the model and to spread devotion to the medal. Stories of cures and conversions made the medals popular and resulted in them being called "miraculous". To spread the devotion, Fr. Aladel formed confraternities or sodalities of the Children of Mary which spread all over the world. A statue of Our Lady of the Miraculous Medal was placed over the main altar in the chapel where Mary appeared to Sr. Catherine.

Feast Day: November 27
Patron Saint of: Universal

Immaculate Heart of Mary

O MOST BLESSED MOTHER,
heart of love, heart of mercy,
ever listening, caring,
consoling, hear our prayer.
As your children, we implore your
intercession with Jesus your Son.
Receive with understanding and
compassion the petitions we place
before you today, especially
(special intention).
We are comforted in knowing your
heart is ever open to those
who ask for your prayer.
We trust to your gentle care and intercession,
those whom we love
and who are sick or lonely or hurting.
Help all of us, Holy Mother to bear
our burdens in this life until we
may share eternal life and peace
with God forever.
Amen.

Immaculate Heart of Mary
HISTORY AND DEVOTION

The Immaculate Heart of Mary is a special form of devotion to the physical heart of Mary. It is Mary's love for God, her love for her Son, and her love for all people that draws us to want to study and to imitate her.

In his Gospel, Luke mentioned the devotion twice, saying that Mary kept what Jesus was saying and doing in her heart.

Historically, during the 12th century, writers such as St. Anselm and St. Bernard of Clairvaux had great influence in Marian devotion.

The Church used the lessons of the Second Nocturn of St. Bernardine of Siena, Doctor of the Heart of Mary, for her feast.

However, it was St. Eudes who renewed the devotion, made it public and published Coeur Admirable (Admirable Heart) to promote devotion to the Immaculate Heart of Mary.

In 1917, at Fatima, Portugal, Mary appeared to three children while in the hills tending sheep.

On July 13, during one of her six apparitions, Mary told the children, "to save poor sinners God wishes to establish in the world devotion to my Immaculate Heart". Twenty-five years later,

December 8, 1942, on the feast of the Immaculate Conception, Pope Pius XII, dedicated the Church and the human race to the Immaculate Heart of Mary and extended the feast to the entire Church.

On March 25, 1984, Pope John Paul II made the solemn act of consecration of the world, particularly Russia, to the Immaculate Heart of Mary. Sister Lucia, the only surviving visionary from the apparitions at Fatima, confirmed that the act of consecration was accepted by Heaven and was fulfilled.

Mary's Immaculate Heart is typically pictured with flames, representing her burning or undying love. Her Heart is encircled by roses or lilies, symbolizing her joys and her purity, and oftentimes, a sword pierces the heart, reflecting the prophesy of Simeon in the Gospel of Luke. Mary's Heart is a symbol of her compassion and her sinlessness.

Feast Day: Saturday after the Solemnity of the Sacred Heart of Jesus (19 days after Pentecost)
Patron Saint of: Philippines

Our Lady of Perpetual Help

O Mother of Perpetual Help, grant that I may
ever invoke Thy most powerful name,
which is the safeguard of the living
and the salvation of the dying.
O Purest Mary, O Sweetest Mary, let Thy name
henceforth be ever on my lips.
Delay not, O Blessed Lady, to help me whenever I
call on Thee, for, in all my needs,
in all my temptations
I shall never cease to call on Thee,
ever repeating Thy sacred name, Mary, Mary.
O what consolation, what sweetness,
what confidence, what emotion
fill my soul when I pronounce
Thy sacred name, or even only think of Thee.
I thank God for having given Thee, for my good,
so sweet, so powerful, so lovely a name.
But I will not be content with merely pronouncing
Thy name: let my love for Thee prompt me
ever to hail Thee, Mother of Perpetual Help.
Recite Nine Hail Mary's.

Our Lady of Perpetual Help
HISTORY AND DEVOTION

The picture of Our Lady of Perpetual Help is said to have been brought from Crete to Rome in the 15th century by a merchant who, upon his dying, asked that Our Lady be placed in a church for public veneration.

The picture was enshrined in St. Matthew Church for 300 years. When the French invaded Rome, St. Matthew's was destroyed, and the Augustinian fathers transferred Our Lady to St. Eusebius. The image was moved to St. Mary of Posterula, where it hung in a side chapel for forty years. In 1853, the Redemptorists built a house in Rome with a small church, St. Alphonsus, adjacent to what was once St. Matthew's. Pope Pius IX asked the Augustinians to give the picture to the Redemptorists and in 1866, during the transfer of Our Lady, a young boy was cured of meningitis and a young girl recovered use of her paralyzed leg. The picture is painted on wood with a gold background in a flat style characteristic of an icon. The Blessed Mother wears a dark red dress with a blue mantle and veil. On the left is the archangel Michael holding a lance and sponge. On the right is the archangel Gabriel holding the cross and nails. The Child Jesus holds his mother's hand with both of his hands and his sandal slips from his foot as he peers at the angels who hold the instruments of his passion. The Greek letters above and below each of the images translate Mother of God, Michael Archangel, Gabriel Archangel and Jesus Christ, respectively. Mary's head gently touches her son's, yet her solemn gaze is toward those who view her. In 1870, the Redemptorists dedicated a small church near Boston to Our Lady of Perpetual Help, receiving from Rome the first copy of the painting touched to the original. Since then over two thousand three hundred copies of the original have been sent out from St. Alphonsus' church in Rome.

Feast Day: June 27
Name Meaning: Forever Helping
Patron Saint of: Italy

Our Lady of Mount Carmel

O Beautiful flower of Carmel,
most fruitful vine,
splendor of Heaven, holy and singular,
who brought forth the Son of God,
still ever remaining a pure virgin,
assist me in my time of need!
(pause and mention petitions)
In you I find consolation
when afflicted,
protection when prosecuted,
strength when burdened with trials,
and light in doubt and darkness.
Dear Lady of Mount Carmel,
I firmly believe that you can grant
me the grace I implore.
My dearest Mary, be pleased to
accept this my act of perfect
resignation to the decrees
of your adorable heart,
which I sincerely desire
to be fulfilled in and by me
and all God's creatures forever.
Amen.

Our Lady of Mount Carmel
HISTORY AND DEVOTION

In the 12th century , the Carmelites lived on Mount Carmel and built the first church dedicated to the Blessed Virgin. They were joined by many pilgrims, established a rule, and became formalized in the 13th century.

The Order spread to Europe and St. Simon became the sixth general in 1245 when the Carmelites government was moved to England from Palestine. On July 16, 1251, in the midst of great persecutions against the Order, St. Simon knelt in prayer to the Blessed Virgin in the convent at Cambridge.

Mary, holding the baby Jesus, appeared to him and handed him the brown scapular, a loose garment worn over the head, down the front and back, from the shoulders to the knees.

She told him to receive the scapular as a sign of a privilege she had obtained for them and all who honored her. It was a "sign of salvation", a "safeguard in danger" and a "special pledge of peace and protection until the end of time".

"Whosoever dies wearing this shall be preserved from eternal flames". The problems that the Carmelites faced ceased and devotion to the scapular spread quickly.

Many miracles have been attached to the wearing of the scapular, and Our Lady chose to include this apparition in two other of her appearances. At Lourdes in 1858, Mary made her last appearance on July 16th, the same day she appeared to St. Simon Stock, and the day the Church celebrates the feast of Our Lady of Mount Carmel. At Fatima in 1917, Mary made her last appearance to the children as Our Lady of Mount Carmel.

Feast Day: July 16
Patron Saint of: Carmelites

Our Lady of the Holy Rosary

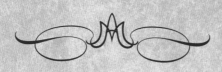

My dearest Mother Mary, behold me, your child, in prayer at your feet. Accept this Holy Rosary, which I offer you in accordance with your requests at Fatima, as a proof of my tender love for you, for the intentions of the Sacred Heart of Jesus, in atonement for the offenses committed against your Immaculate Heart, and for this special favor which I earnestly request in my Rosary Novena:

(Mention your request).

I beg you to present my petition to your Divine Son. If you will pray for me, I cannot be refused. I know, dearest Mother, that you want me to seek God's holy Will concerning my request. If what I ask for should not be granted, pray that I may receive that which will be of greater benefit to my soul.

I offer you this spiritual "Bouquet of Roses" because I love you. I put all my confidence in you, since your prayers before God are most powerful. For the greater glory of God and for the sake of Jesus, your loving Son, hear and grant my prayer.

Sweet Heart of Mary, be my salvation.

Our Lady of the Holy Rosary
HISTORY AND DEVOTION

The feast of Our Lady of the Rosary was first established by Pope Pius V in 1573 in thanksgiving to God for the Christian armada's defeat of the Turkish fleet at Lepanto.

Pope Clement XI extended the feast to the entire Church in 1716 after the Christian defeat of the Turks in Hungary. The rosary is said to have developed through the early Christian practice of reciting the 150 Psalms prayed by the Church. Those unable to read replaced the Psalms with 150 Our Fathers, using what was referred to as paternoster beads for counting, and eventually with 150 Hail Marys, also called Our Lady's Psalter. In 1208, Domingo de Guzman, a Spanish preacher, went to France to defend the faith against the Albigensian heresy.

As Dominic prayed in the chapel in Prouille, Our Lady appeared to him and taught him the complete rosary, attaching 15 promises for those who prayed the rosary faithfully.

These promises include special protection and graces, a decrease in sin, an abundance of mercy for souls, and reception of the sacraments before dying.

St. Dominic founded the Dominican Friars, opened monasteries, and spread devotion to the rosary all over the world.

In 1917, Our Lady appeared in Fatima, Portugal to three children, Jacinta, Francisco and Lucia as they were tending sheep.

During the sixth apparition on October 13, Our Lady told the children that she wanted a chapel built there in her honor and she wanted people to pray the rosary daily. She told the children, "I am the Lady of the Rosary".

Feast Day: October 7
Patron Saint of: Universal

Our Lady of Sorrows

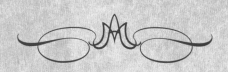

O Mother of Sorrows, by the anguish and
love with which thou didst stand at the
Cross of Jesus, stand by me in my last agony.
To thy maternal heart I commend
the last three hours of my life.
Offer these hours to the Eternal Father in
union with the agony of our dearest Lord
in atonement for my sins.
Offer to the Eternal Father the most Precious
Blood of Jesus, mingled with your
tears on Calvary, that I may obtain the
grace of receiving Holy Communion with
the most perfect love and contrition before
my death, and that I may breathe
forth my soul in the adorable presence of Jesus.
Dearest Mother, when the moment of my
death has at length come, present me as
your child to Jesus. Ask Him to forgive me
for having offended Him for I know not what I did.
Beg Him to receive me into His Kingdom
of glory to be united with Him forever.
Amen.

Our Lady of Sorrows
HISTORY AND DEVOTION

Our Lady of Sorrows, or Mater Dolorosa, is the title given to the Blessed Virgin Mary referring to the sufferings she endured as the Mother of Jesus.

The feast of Our Lady of Sorrows was first celebrated in 1244 by the seven founders of the Servite Order to help them focus their devotion and meditation on the Sorrows of Mary.

Standing under the cross was the principal devotion of their order.

Since the 14th century there are traditionally seven sorrows that have been honored: the Prophecy of Simeon (Luke 2:25-35), the Flight into Egypt (Matthew 2:13-15), the Loss of the Child Jesus for Three Days (Luke 2:41-50), Mary meets Jesus on the Way to Calvary (John 19:17), Mary watches the Crucifixion and Death of Jesus (John 19:25-30), Mary receives the Body of Jesus down from the Cross (John 19: 31-37) and Mary watches as Jesus is Laid in the Tomb (John 19:38-42).

The feast of Our Lady of Sorrows is dedicated to Mary's suffering and grief in union with her Son. In her compassion for the sufferings of her Son, she shows the depth of her love as Mother.

The image of Our Lady of Sorrows is traditionally shown dressed in black with seven swords piercing her heart. Each sword depicting a chief sorrow that Mary suffered in union with her Son.

The sword piercing Mary's heart is also seen in the biblical reference, Luke 2:35, where Simeon tells her that she herself would be pierced by a sword so that the thoughts of many hearts would be laid bare.

Feast Day: September 15
Patron Saint of: Universal

Our Lady of
Częstochowa

(To be said each day upon arising)
Holy Mother of Czestochowa,
Thou art full of grace,
goodness and mercy.
I consecrate to Thee all my thoughts,
words and actions
my soul and body.
I beseech Thy blessings and
especially prayers for my salvation.
Today, I consecrate myself to Thee,
Good Mother, totally
with body and soul amid joy
and sufferings to obtain for myself
and others Thy blessings on this earth
and eternal life in Heaven.
Amen.

Our Lady of Czestochowa
HISTORY AND DEVOTION

Our Lady of Czestochowa, according to tradition, is a sacred icon believed to be painted by St. Luke the Evangelist on the top of a table built by Jesus. As St. Luke painted, he listened to Mary tell of the life of her Son; information he used later in writing his Gospel. St. Helena moved the painting from Jerusalem to Constantinople, where it was enthroned in a Church. It was given as a gift to the Princess of Ruthenia and brought to Poland in 1382 by St. Ladislaus after an arrow scarred the Blessed Virgin's throat during an attack by the Tartars. While taking the painting to his birthplace, Opala, through Czestochowa, the horses pulling the wagon stopped and would not move. Accepting this as a sign from the Blessed Virgin, Ladislaus founded a monastery of Pauline Fathers to protect the icon and placed the image in the Church of the Assumption.

During an invasion by the Hussites, the portrait was broken in three pieces and struck by a sword, causing two deep slashes in Mary's cheek.

In 1655, monks begged the icon for deliverance against the Swedes and despite being outnumbered, Poland defeated the enemy.

King Jan Casimir proclaimed the Mother of God to be the Queen of the Polish Crown.

In 1717, Pope Clement XI acknowledged the miracles associated to the icon.

In 1920, when the Soviet army arrived at the banks of the River Vistula, the people prayed to Our Lady. The next day, the feast of Our Lady of Sorrows, the Russian army withdrew after the image of Mary appeared in the clouds above the city. Despite the German capture of Poland during World War II, thousands of pilgrims secretly journeyed to visit the image and implored her protection. The icon of Our Lady of Czestochowa is enshrined on Jasna Gora, above the city of Czestochowa in South Central Poland. The miraculous image is one of the oldest pictures of the Blessed Virgin in the world.

Feast Day: August 26
Patron Saint of: Poland

Our Lady of Good Counsel

O Holy Virgin, to whose feet we are led by our anxious
uncertainty in our search for and attainment of what
is true and good, invoking you by the sweet title of
Mother of Good Counsel, we beseech you to come to
our assistance, when, along the road of this life, the
darkness of error and of evil conspires towards our
ruin by leading our minds and our hearts astray.
O Seat of Wisdom and Star of the Sea, enlighten the
doubtful and the erring, that they be not seduced by
the false appearances of good; render them steadfast
in the face of the hostile and corrupting influences of
passion and of sin, O Mother of Good Counsel, obtain
for us from your Divine Son a great love of virtue, and,
in the hour of uncertainty and trial, the strength to
embrace the way that leads to our salvation.
If your hand sustains us, we shall walk unmolested
along the path indicated to us by the life and words of
Jesus, our Redeemer; and having followed freely and
securely, even in the midst of this world's strife, the
Sun of Truth and Justice under your maternal Star,
we shall come to the enjoyment of full and eternal
peace with you in the haven of salvation. Amen.

Composed by Pope Pius XII (Pont. 1939-1958)

Our Lady of Good Counsel
HISTORY AND DEVOTION

In the fifth century, the small town of Genazzano, southeast of Rome, contributed a large sum of money to Pope Sixtus III for the restoration of St. Mary Major in Rome.

In appreciation, a Church was built in Genazzano and entrusted to the care of the Augustinian Fathers. As time passed, the church was in need of large repairs. With no help from the town, a local widow, Petruccia de Geneo, donated all of her savings for the restoration, but was unable to finish to project.

On St. Mark's Day, April 25, 1467, a crowd of people witnessed as a cloud descended upon the unfinished church. The church bells began to ring on their own, and as the cloud moved, it revealed a portrait of Mary that came to rest on a narrow ledge near an unfinished wall in the church. The painting, now known as Our Lady of Good Counsel, is on a thin layer of plaster as thin as an egg shell, and is suspended without support.

Two weeks after the event, two refugees from Albania arrived in the town and testified that the same painting was in a church in Albania a few weeks earlier but disappeared when the town was invaded. Upon checking their story, an empty space the size of the picture was left in the plaster of a church at Scutari in Albania.

Because of the miraculous event, the church in Genazzano was completed and pilgrimages began. In the first six months, over 170 miracles were recorded. In 1727, Pope Benedict XIII granted an Office and Mass of Our Lady of Good Counsel for April 25th, but it is celebrated a day later to avoid conflict with the feast of St. Mark.

Feast Day: April 26
Patron Saint: Albania, diocese of Essen, Germany, enlightenment, diocese of Sandhurst, Victoria

Our Lady of Mercy

Blessed Virgin Mary,
who can worthily repay you with praise
and thanks for having rescued a fallen world
by your generous consent! Receive our gratitude
and by your prayers obtain the pardon of our sins.
Take our prayers into the sanctuary of Heaven
and enable them to make our peace with God.
Holy Mary, help the miserable,
strengthen the discouraged.
Comfort the sorrowful, pray for your people,
plead for the clergy,
intercede for all women consecrated to God.
May all who venerate you
feel now your help and protection.
Be ready to help us when we pray,
and bring back to us the answers to our prayers.
Make it your continual concern
to pray for the people of God,
for you were blessed by God
and were made worthy to bear
the Redeemer of the world,
Who lives and reigns forever.
Amen.
St. Augustine

Our Lady of Mercy
History and Devotion

In 1218, the Blessed Mother appeared to St. Peter Nolasco with this message, "Find for me other men like yourself, an army of brave, generous, unselfish men, and send them into the lands where the children of the Faith are suffering". Peter had been working for several years trying to ransom the Christian captives taken by the Saracens or Moors for slaves.

He was very devoted to Christ and to the Blessed Virgin Mary.

When Peter asked Our Lady who was talking to him, she revealed herself as Mary, the Mother of God.

She asked Peter, St. Raymond of Pennafort and King James of Aragon to establish an Order dedicated to visiting and to freeing Christians in captivity. She was dressed in white with the shield of the Order imprinted on her scapular.

Following Our Lady's request, the Mercedarian Order was constituted in Barcelona by King James. Pope Gregory IX approved the Order in 1235 with Peter as the first superior.

Many of the new Order were religious who prayed and collected alms for the Christians in captivity.

The other group in the Order were knights who actually went to the camps to buy back the Christians, or to trade places with them, securing their freedom.

As well as Our Lady of Mercy, Mary was also given the name Our Lady of Ransom upon this apparition. She is often pictured holding two bags of coins to symbolize the ransom paid.

Thousands of Christian prisoners were freed by this Order.

Feast Day: September 24
Patron Saint of: Barcelona

Our Lady Star of the Sea

Stella Maris

Hail, bright star of ocean,
God's own Mother blest,
Ever sinless Virgin,
Gate of heavenly rest,
Taking that sweet Ave,
Which from Gabriel came,
Peace confirm within us,
Changing Eva's name,
Break the captive's fetters,
Light on blindness pure,
All our ills expelling,
Every bliss implore,
Show thyself a Mother,
May the Word divine,
Born for us thine infant,
Hear our prayers through thine.
Virgin all excelling,
Mildest of the mild,
Freed from guilt preserve us,
Meek and undefiled,
Keep our life all spotless,
Make our way secure,
Till we find in Jesus,
Joy forevermore.
Through the highest Heaven
To the almighty Three,
Father, Son and Spirit
One some glory be.

Our Lady
Star of the Sea
HISTORY AND DEVOTION

Our Lady, Star of the Sea is the title given to Mary emphasizing her role as a sign of hope and guidance for those who travel or work on the sea.

As her Son accompanied His disciples in their boats, aided them in their livelihoods, and calmed the storms at sea, so too Mary is called upon for protection by seafarers.

In the Biblical passage 1 Kings 18:41-45, there is a cloud above the sea seen from Mount Carmel that is no bigger than a man's hand.

A tiny cloud believed to be the "Star of the Sea" is a sign of hope to end a long drought.

Around the year 400, St. Jerome interprets the Hebrew name of Mary as "stella maris" (a drop in the sea). In his encyclical on the last Doctor of the Church, St. Bernard of Clairvaux, Pope Pius XII quotes him saying, "Mary… is interpreted to mean 'Star of the Sea.'"

This admirably befits the Virgin Mother… as the ray does not diminish the brightness of the star, so neither did the Child born of her tarnish the beauty of Mary's virginity."

Mary, as the guiding star, has led to the devotion to Our Lady, Star of the Sea.

She is the patroness of the Catholic missions to seafarers, the Apostleship of the Sea, and to many coastal churches and communities.

Feast Day: September 27
Patron Saint: sailors, navigators, yachtsmen, seafarers

Rosa Mystica

Rosa Mystica, Immaculate Virgin,
Mother of Grace, in honor of thy Divine Son,
we prostrate ourselves at thy feet to implore God's mercy.
We beg for help and grace, not relying on any merit of
ours, but on the kindness of thy motherly heart,
and confident that thou will grant our urgent requests.
Hail Mary...
Rose Mystica, Mother of Jesus,
Queen of the Holy Rosary and Mother of the Church,
of the Mystical Body of Christ,
we implore the gifts of unity and peace
for the anxious world, and those graces so able
to convert the souls of thy erring children.
Hail Mary...
Rosa Mystica, Queen of the Apostles,
pray that many men and women may hear
Christ's call to priestly and religious vocations,
and help them spread the Kingdom of Jesus Christ
throughout the world by the holiness of their lives
and their burning zeal for the salvation of souls.
Pour out thy Heavenly grace upon us!
Hail Mary...

Mystical Rose
History and Devotion

In the Spring of 1947, the Blessed Mother appeared to Pierina Gilli, a nurse in the hospital at Montichiari in Northern Italy. Our Lady was dressed in mauve and her heart was pierced with three swords.

She simply asked for prayer, sacrifice and penance. During a second apparition on July 13th, Mary appeared in a white dress and the swords were replaced by a white, a red and a yellow rose.

She revealed Our Lord's desire of Marian Devotion by all priests, nuns and religious orders.

Mary promised to protect religious orders who venerated her.

She asked that July 13th be celebrated in honor of the Rosa Mystica. In the 6th apparition, Jacinta and Francesco from the apparition in Fatima, appeared on either side of Our Lady to re-emphasize the messages given there.

In the seventh apparition on December 8th, Mary revealed "I am the Immaculate Conception. I wish people to celebrate each year on December 8th, at noon, the hour of grace for the world."

As the apparitions moved from the hospital to the church, the faithful came to the church for prayer and for healing.

A young boy with polio and an older girl with severe tuberculosis were cured completely.

Our Lady's requests under the title of Rosa Mystica continued in 1966 at Fontanelle, just outside of Montichiari.

Mary blessed the spring of water there and asked that all in the village "do acts of charity for the sick who will come there."

Pilgrims come from all over the world to venerate Mary as the Rosa Mystica.

Our Lady
Help of Christians

Most Holy Virgin Mary, Help of Christians,
how sweet it is to come
to your feet imploring your perpetual help.
If earthly mothers cease
not to remember their children, how can you,
the most loving of all mothers forget me?
Grant then to me, I implore you,
your perpetual help in all my necessities,
in every sorrow,
and especially in all my temptations.
I ask for your unceasing help
for all who are now suffering.
Help the weak, cure the sick, convert sinners.
Grant through your intercessions
many vocations to the religious life.
Obtain for us, O Mary, Help of Christians,
that having invoked you on earth
we may love and eternally thank you in Heaven.

By St. John Bosco

Our Lady Help of Christians
HISTORY AND DEVOTION

Saint John Chrysostom first used the title Help of Christians to refer to Mary in a homily in 345. St. Don Bosco dedicated the mother church at Turin of the Salesian Congregation to Our Lady Help of Christians in 868.

The devotion became popular in 1572 when Pope Pius V asked Christian armies to pray to Mary to help the Christians against the Ottoman Empire.

Through the intercession of Our Lady Help of Christians, the Turks were defeated.

In 1808, by order of Napoleon, Pope Pius VII was arrested and imprisoned.

After six years, and at the end of the Battle of Leipzig, Pope Pius VII was taken back to Savona and released.

This was on the eve of the feast of Our Lady of Mercy, Patroness of Savona. He would return later to crown her image.

His journey back to Rome was a victory march for the Church attributed to the Blessed Mother. He visited many of Our Lady's sanctuaries along the way and crowned her images.

Pope Pius entered Rome May 24, 1814, to

cheers from people who crowded the streets awaiting his return.

To give thanks to God and to Mary, he instituted the Feast of Our Lady, Help of Christians to be celebrated May 24th.

Feast Day: May 24
Patron Saint: Australia, Andorran security forces, New York, New Zealand

Our Lady
Queen of the Angels

August Queen of Heaven!
sovereign queen of Angels,
you who at the beginning received from God
the power and the mission
to crush the head of Satan,
we beseech you humbly,
send your holy legions so that,
on your orders and by your power,
they will track down demons,
fight them everywhere,
curb their audacity and plunge them into the abyss.
Who can be compared to God?
Oh good and tender Mother,
you will always be our love and our hope.
Oh divine Mother,
send the Holy Angels and Archangels to defend me,
and to keep the cruel enemy far from me.
Holy Angels and Archangels defend us,
protect us.

Amen.

Our Lady
Queen of the Angels
HISTORY AND DEVOTION

ary is given the title Queen of the Angels because she is favored by God above all, even the Angels.

In tradition we know that angels sing His praises and are messengers of God but we know that Mary is more than a messenger.

The angels, too, are servants of God but Mary is more than a servant.

She is His Mother and in the Heavenly Kingdom, Queen of the Angels.

From the beginning to the end, angels played a major role in the life of the Blessed Virgin Mary.

The Angel Gabriel announced to Mary that she had been chosen to be the Mother of our Savior. An angel appeared to Joseph and explained that he was to take Mary as his wife.

The angels appeared to the shepherds to announce the birth of Jesus and instructed Joseph to avoid Herod.

We envision a host of angels escorting Mary into Heaven and gathering around her as she is crowned Queen.

Pope Pius XII explained that "all paradise recognized that Mary was worthy of receiving honor and glory and queenship because she is full of grace, and also because she is holier and more beautiful than the greatest saints and angels, individually, or taken together."

It is that Mary is the Mother of Jesus and reigns higher in sanctity than all of the angels, that they accept and love her as Queen.

Feast Day: August 2
Patron Saint: Costa Rica

Our Lady of La Salette

Remember, Our Lady of La Salette, true Mother
of Sorrows, the tears you shed for us on Calvary.
Remember also the care you have taken to keep us
faithful to Christ, your Son.
Having done so much for your children,
you will not now abandon us.
Comforted by this consoling thought,
we come to you pleading,
despite our infidelities and ingratitude.
Virgin of Reconciliation,
do not reject our prayers, but intercede for us,
obtain for us the grace to love Jesus above all else.
May we console you by living a holy life
and so come to share the eternal life Christ
gained by his cross.
Amen.

La Salette Invocation
Our Lady of La Salette, Reconciler of sinners,
pray without ceasing for us who have recourse to you.

Our Lady of La Salette
HISTORY AND DEVOTION

On September 19, 1846, in the parish of La Salette in the French Alps, Mary appeared to two young children, Melanie Mathieu, age 14, and Maximin Giraud, age 11. The children were tending cows when they decided to take a nap. As they awoke, they realized that the cows had strayed. Searching for them, they noticed a bright light, "much brighter than the sun", and as they crossed a dried up stream they saw in the light a beautiful lady seated with her head in her hands.

As they approached, they could see tears streaming down her face.

She told the children that they were to spread the message: "If my people will not submit I shall be forced to let go the hand of my Son. It is so strong, so heavy, that I can no longer withhold it."

She told them that unless people repented, the crops would fail, and there would be a great famine. She explained that she was holding back the hand of her Son with her prayers for the people who worked on Sundays, did not attend Mass, and used God's name in vain.

She asked them to pray at least an Our Father or a Hail Mary at night and in the morning.

She left as quietly as she had come, and the children rushed to the village to tell their stories.

Despite opposition, the children delivered the messages given from Our Lady, and after four years the apparition was approved.

In 1879, the Basilica of Our Lady of La Salette was built where Mary appeared. The stream which now flows through the ravine has been the source of many cures, and the area is a major site for pilgrimages.

Feast Day: September 19
Patron Saint of: Palermo, El Hatillo

Our Lady of Loreto

O Mary, Immaculate Virgin, for the sake of your
blessed house, which we the angels moved
to the pleasant hills of Loreto,
turn your benevolent eyes toward us.
For the holy walls within which you were born and
lived as a child, with prayers and the most sublime
love; for the fortunate walls that listened to the
greetings of the angel who called you; "Blessed among
all women", and which remind us of the incarnation
of the word in your purest bosom; for your blessed house,
where you lived with Jesus and Joseph, and which
became during the centuries the fervently longed-for
destination of the saints, who considered themselves
lucky to kiss fervently your sacred walls, bestow upon
us the graces which we humbly ask, and the fortune of
coming to Heaven after the exile, to repeat to you the
greetings of the angel: Hail Mary.

50 days of indulgence are bestowed to everyone who
will recite this prayer.

Our Lady of Loreto
HISTORY AND DEVOTION

The title, Our Lady of Loreto, refers the image of Mary associated with the Holy House of Loreto. In 1291, tradition says that angels transported the house, where Mary was born and where the Annunciation occurred, from the Holy Land to Tersato, Dalmatia (Yugoslavia) to preserve it from being demolished during the Crusades.

Shepherds, knowing their land quite well, discovered the sudden arrival of the small house in their fields.

They immediately told the local priest who himself was severely crippled, but made the effort to go and spend time inside the house.

After he received in a vision information about the house, he was cured of his long time illness.

The priest was told that the altar was put there by St. Peter and the figure of Mary, now Our Lady of Loreto, was carved by St. Luke (since replaced due to damage to the original).

The head of the city sent a group to the Holy Land, who discovered that the house where Mary was born was missing.

The foundation left behind measured exactly the length and width of the walls now in Tersato.

In 1294, the house was said to be moved by angels to a forest in Reananti, Italy, near the Adriatic Sea. As villains began to rob pilgrims on their way through the woods, the house was moved to Loreto, Italy.

Because of the transportation of the house by flight, Our Lady is known as the patroness of aviation.

She is also known as the patroness of builders and construction workers since the house still stands strong with no foundation.

Feast Day: December 10
Patron Saint of: aviation, pilots, builders, construction workers, flyers, Loreto

Our Lady
Queen of Peace

Most holy and immaculate Virgin,
Mother of Jesus and our loving Mother,
being His Mother,
you shared in His universal kingship.
The prophets and angels proclaimed Him King of peace.
With loving fervor in our hearts
we salute and honor you as Queen of peace.

We pray that your intercession
may protect us and all people from hatred and discord,
and direct our hearts into the ways of peace and justice
which your Son taught and exemplified.
We ask your maternal care for our Holy Father
who works to reconcile the nations in peace.
We seek your guidance for our Head of State
and other leaders as they strive for world peace.

Glorious Queen of peace,
grant us peace in our hearts,
harmony in our families
and concord throughout the world.
Immaculate Mother,
as patroness of our beloved country,
watch over us and protect us
with your motherly love.

Amen.

Our Lady Queen of Peace

HISTORY AND DEVOTION

Our Lady Queen of Peace is the title given to Mary as patroness of the Congregation of the Sacred Hearts of Jesus and Mary.

During the French Revolution (1789-1799), Fr. Peter Coudrin hid in an attic for six months where he had a vision of being surrounded by groups of priests and sisters in white robes.

He believed this to be a sign from God of a religious order he was to establish.

He began his underground ministry in Poitiers. In 1794, he met Henriette Aymer de Chevalerie after she was released from prison for hiding a priest.

She shared with Fr. Peter a vision she had similar to his vision of groups of priests and sisters dressed in white robes.

Together, in 1800, they officially established the Congregation of the Sacred Hearts of Jesus and Mary. Founding new schools for poor children and seminaries, they spread the message of God's unconditional love and mercy.

In 1827 they organized teams of missionaries to spread the Gospel to the Pacific Islands.

Establishing the Roman Catholic Diocese of Honolulu, they built the Cathedral of Our Lady of Peace and consecrated the islands under her protection.

It is one of the oldest Roman Cathedrals in continuous use in the United States.

Her memorial feast is celebrated on January 24th in Hawaii, and July 9th in other areas, because the Archbishop of Paris crowned the original statue on that date in 1906.

Feast Day: July 9
Patron Saint: Congregation of the Sacred Hearts of Jesus and Mary

Our Lady of the Highway

O Lady of the Highway,
be with us on our journey,
for all your ways are beautiful
and all your paths are peace.
O God, Who with unspeakable
providence does rule and govern
the world, grant unto us, Your servants,
through the intercessions
of our watchful mother,
to be protected from all danger
and brought safely to the
end of our journey.
Amen.

Our Lady of the Highway

HISTORY AND DEVOTION

The title of Mary as Our Lady of the Highway comes from the many prolonged travels Mary endured during her lifetime.

In the Gospel of Luke, Mary goes to visit Elizabeth "proceeding in haste into the hill country to a town of Judah." Luke then recounts the travels due to the census, "and so Joseph went from the town of Nazareth in Galilee to Judea, to David's town of Bethlehem to register with Mary, his espoused wife, who was with child."

On this particular journey, Mary and Joseph must find a place to stay the night and a place to give birth to their newborn Son. Mary and Joseph later take Jesus to Jerusalem to "present him to the Lord" and they return to Nazareth. Then, they travel back to Jerusalem with Him at the age of twelve for the feast of Passover and have to search for Him when they were already on the road back home.

This concludes with the important message of Jesus' staying behind to "be in his Father's house."

Matthew's Gospel tells of the young couple's flight to Egypt to avoid Herod and back to Nazareth.

He then proceeds to tell of Mary's travels with her Son during his ministry and finally the long journey with Him to Calvary.

Mary, as Our Lady of the Highway, is called upon to watch over us in our travels as she watched over the Holy Family in their travels.

There are many shrines to Our Lady of the Highway calling upon her for safety and for protection.

Patron Saint of: travel

Our Lady
Queen of the Universe

Mary, Queen of the Universe, you are a Queen
in that you are Mother of the Word Incarnate.
Christ is universal King in that He rules all
His creatures by His personal union
with the Father and the Spirit.
He is King and you are Queen of all hearts.
Rule over us by the queenly power of your love
that the Kingdom of your Son;
the Kingdom of truth and life,
holiness and grace, justice and love,
and peace may come upon the earth.

Grant your graces to all people, The Holy Spirit
for the whole Church, and peace for the entire earth.
Amen.

The Immaculate Virgin,
preserved free from all guilt of original sin,
on the completion of her earthly sojourn,
was taken up body and soul into heavenly glory,
and exalted by the Lord as Queen of the Universe,
that she might be the more fully conformed to her Son,
the Lord of lords and the conqueror of sin and death.

(Vatican II, L.G. 59)

Our Lady Queen of the Universe

History and Devotion

According to ancient tradition, the royal dignity of Mary rests in her Divine Motherhood.

In Luke's Gospel we read, "He shall be called the Son of the Most High, and the Lord God shall give unto him the throne of David, his father, and he shall reign in the house of Jacob forever, and of his kingdom there will be no end."

Mary is also referred to as "the Mother of the Lord", thus a Queen.

The early writers of the Church refer to Mary as "the Mother of the King of the Universe," therefore, Queen of the Universe and "the Virgin Mother who brought forth the King of the whole world."

St. John Damascene writes, "When she became Mother of the Creator, she truly became Queen of every creature."

In the final book of Revelation we read, "A great sign appeared in the sky, a woman clothed with the sun, with the moon under her feet, and on her head a crown of twelve stars."

Because of Jesus' close relationship to His Mother, we understand that she shares in His kingship.

As in the final Coronation, Mary is crowned Queen of Heaven and Earth, Queen of the Universe.

Feast Day: August 22

Our Lady of the Sacred Heart

Remember, Our Lady of the Sacred Heart,
the ineffable power which your Divine Son
has given you over His adorable Heart.
Full of confidence in your merits,
we now implore your protection.
O Heavenly Treasurer of the Heart of Jesus,
of that Heart which is the inexhaustible source
of all graces and which you do open
when it pleases you,
in order to distribute among men
all the treasures of love and mercy,
of light and salvation which it contains: grant us,
we beseech you, the favors we request,
(Mention you requests.)
No, we cannot meet with a refusal,
and since you are our Mother,
Our Lady of the Sacred Heart,
favorably hear and grant our prayers.
Amen.

Our Lady of the Sacred Heart

HISTORY AND DEVOTION

Our Lady of the Sacred Heart is the title given to Mary by the founder of the Missionaries of the Sacred Heart, Jules Chevalier. As an assistant priest at Issoudun, France, Jules told another assistant priest about his dream to start a new Order.

Together they prayed and asked God for a sign that they should move forward. The novena ended on December 8, 1854, and on that same day the two priests were told that twenty thousand francs had been given by a charitable person for them to establish a good work.

The archbishop would not give approval of the new Order until the priests could continue with a regular income. Nine days before the Feast of the Immaculate Heart, the two priests promised Mary that they would dedicate the new Order to the Heart of Jesus and the Immaculate Heart of Mary, and make them known throughout the world.

At the end of the nine days, another person promised one thousand francs per year for the priests to live on.

The Archbishop was satisfied, but his Council rejected the proposal, saying that the priests were too young to start such an organization and maintain it. Jules was asked to forget the pursuit but He continued to pray to the Blessed Mother.

The Archbishop finally went over the Council and authorized the two priests to start the Missionaries of the Sacred Heart. They soon became the clergy of the archdiocese.

Fr. Jules worked for several years on how he would honor the Blessed Virgin Mary. He put the devotion of the Sacred Heart and Mary together in the title, "Our Lady of the Sacred Heart".

Feast Day: May 31
Patron Saint: Missionaries of the Sacred Heart

Our Lady of Knock

My Queen! My Mother!

I give you all myself,

and, to show my devotion to you,

I consecrate to you my eyes, my ears,

my mouth, my heart, my entire self.

Wherefore, O loving Mother,

as I am your own, keep me, defend me,

as your property and possession.

Our Lady of Knock
History and Devotion

On August 21, 1879, Mary McLoughlin, the housekeeper for the small parish church in County Mayo, Ireland, went to visit a friend.

As she walked past the chapel, she noticed a bright light shadowing what looked like three figures she guessed were new statues that the priest had purchased.

After a short visit, Mary McLoughlin and Mary Byrne walked back to the rectory in the rain.

As they approached, they saw against the gable wall actual people: Mary, St. Joseph and St. John. Our Lady was looking toward Heaven with her hands slightly raised.

Mary Byrne left Mary McLoughlin there and ran to tell her family. Eighteen people, ranging from six to seventy years old, came and witnessed the vision. Mary was in the center wearing white with a large crown on her head.

St. Joseph was on her right and had his head slightly toward her. St. John was on her left with his hand raised, as if giving a blessing.

There was a lamb resting on an altar behind them. The next day, many of the villagers went to the priest and reported the apparition.

Word spread, and pilgrims arrived in Knock by the thousands.

In 1880, a statue of Our Lady of Knock was erected where the vision occurred. Many cures have been reported and the Church noted the apparition as probable in 1971.

In 1976, a new church was dedicated to Our Lady, and in 1979 Pope John Paul II made a pilgrimage to Knock.

She is also known as Our Lady of Silence.

Feast Day: Saturday following the second Sunday
after pentecost
Patron Saint of: Ireland

Our Lady of San Juan

Oh most holy and immaculate Virgin of San Juan,
be our faithful companion on our life's journey.

We thank you because many
have found in this Shrine a
place where we feel at home
with you and with our brothers
and sisters.

Help us to come closer to your Son, Jesus;
that we may find in Him the Way of life which
gives meaning to moments of sorrow
and happiness in our earthly pilgrimage.

Our Lady of San Juan
HISTORY AND DEVOTION

In 1542, a Spanish priest brought a small statue of the Virgin of the Immaculate Conception to the village of San Juan Metzquititlan Baptiste, Mexico. He intended to use the small figure to promote the teachings of the Immaculate Conception.

In 1623, a group of acrobats came to perform in the town. They placed swords on the ground to heighten the excitement of their act.

During the standard routine, their six year old daughter fell and, pierced by the swords, was mortally injured.

She was taken to the Chapel of Our Lady of San Juan and the caretaker's wife asked the family to pray that Our Lady would save her.

They prayed before the image and the young girl recovered without a single scar left on her body. Grateful to Our Lady, the father took the deteriorating statue, made of cornstalks and glue, to a local artist for repair. After returning the statue to the Chapel, he went back to pay the artist for his work but the man was nowhere to be found.

That same year, the town changed its name to San Juan de los Lagos.

The statue immediately began to be venerated and pilgrims came from all over praying and seeking cures and favors. With the pilgrims came a steady flow of gifts and construction of a Church began in 1732.

The Virgin, only 12-15 inches high, was installed in 1769. As time went on, the Church was recognized as a Basilica in 1972.

Thousands of pilgrims journey to the shrine each year at the end of January and the beginning of February.

Many make promises to walk from all over Mexico in exchange for the healing of their loved ones. San Juan de los Lagos is the second most visited shrine in Mexico.

Feast Day: December 8
Patron Saint: Saint Juan

Caridad del Cobre

Our Lady of Charity

N. S. DE LA CARIDAD DEL COBRE

Most Holy Mother of Charity
who came to us as a messenger of peace across the sea.
You are the Mother of all Cubans.
To you we come, Most Holy Mother of God
to honor you with love as your children.
To your motherly heart
we entrust our desires and hopes
our work and our prayers.
We pray for our torn country
that we may be able to build
a nation based on peace and unity.
We pray for our families
that they may live in fidelity and love.

We pray for our children
that they may grow strong
in spirit and in body.
We pray for our young people
that their faith may increase,
as well as their attachment to
the truth.

We pray for the sick, the homeless,
the lonely, the exiled,
and for all suffering souls.
We pray for the Catholic Church in Cuba,
for its mission,
for its priests, deacons,
religious and laity.

We pray for the victory
of justice and love
in our country.

Mother of Charity!
We place ourselves
under your mantle of protection!
Blessed are you among women
and blessed is the fruit of your womb, Jesus!
And to Him be the glory and the power
now and forever. Amen.

Caridad del Cobre
HISTORY AND DEVOTION

In the early 1600's, two brothers, Rodrigo and Juan de Hoyos, and their slave, Juan Moreno, together now known as the "three Juans", set out to the Bay of Nipe for the salt mines.

Their village of Barajagua needed the salt to preserve the meat at the slaughter house so they could supply the workers and their families.

After a violent storm which could have completely destroyed their small boat, the three could see a white bundle in the distance floating in the water on a piece of wood.

The waves brought a statue of the Blessed Mother holding the Child Jesus to them.

On the board was writing that translated, "I am the Virgin of Charity."

All three noticed that although the statue had been floating around in the splashing waves, it was completely dry.

They returned to Santiago del Prado, now known as El Cobre, and brought the statue to their village of Barajagua. A chapel was built to venerate the image of Our Lady who the locals believed was a symbol of their Mother caring for and standing beside her children.

In 1916, Pope Benedict XV declared Our Lady of Charity patroness of Cuba at the request of the veterans of Cuba's War of Independence from Spain. The sanctuary of Our Lady was raised to the category of Basilica in 1977 by Pope Paul VI.

Feast Day: September 8
Patron Saint of: Cuba

Our Lady
of Providence

God, our Father,
we give you thanks as we honor
the Blessed Virgin Mary,
Mother of Divine Providence.
Through the power of the Holy Spirit,
She became the mother of the Savior.
As queen sitting at the right hand of her Son,
she aids the Church in her needs and
with maternal care provides for the personal needs
of her children who were entrusted to her
at the Cross by Jesus, our Lord.
We implore you Father, through the prayers
of our Lady, Mother of Divine Providence,
to remove from us whatever is harmful,
and to bestow on us
only that which will be helpful.
We ask you this through Christ our Lord.

Our Lady of Providence
History and Devotion

Our Lady of Providence is associated with the history of the first Barnabite house in Rome. In 1611, the Barnabites, clerics regular of St. Paul, were unable to finish the construction of the Church of St. Charles at Catinari due to financial problems. The pastor made a pilgrimage to Loreto to beg Our Lady for help. Upon his return, his prayers were answered and he received the financial means to complete the Church.

To guarantee that Our Lady receive credit for the miracle, the pastor placed a factual account of Mary's intervention in the parish archives. In 1663, during some renovation work, an image of Our Lady was moved to a place in the Church over the altar.

After it fell and broke into pieces, the architect offered the Barnabites a beautiful painting of the Blessed Mother with the Child Jesus in her lap by the artist Gaetan.

One of the Fathers found the writings of the original pastor and was moved by the trust and devotion he showed toward Our Lady, now known as Our Lady, Mother of Providence.

Devotion to Our Lady passed to Spain where a shrine was built in Tarragona, Catalonia. A Catalan priest, named bishop of Puerto Rico, was assigned a diocese in ruin due to financial difficulties.

Putting everything in the hands of Our Lady, the Cathedral was restored and the diocese reestablished. Symbolic is the way the Child's fingers wrap around Our Lady's hand. "Mother, I place in your hands the authority to act in my name. From my infinite treasure, you are to provide good things to all those who implore your aid."

Feast Day: November 19
Patron Saint of: Puerto Rico

Our Lady
of Regla

O Mary,
Virgin of the rule,
from your shrine in Opon,
and others around the world,
you pour upon all the blessings from God.
Grant that as we invoke you
we may always experience
your powerful protection;
so that guided by your light,
You who are the shining lighthouse
in the ocean of God's mercy,
and inspired by your life - the rule and norm
of ours - we may reach the port of salvation,
through Jesus Christ, Our Lord,
Amen.

Our Lady of Regla
History and Devotion

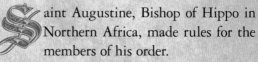

Saint Augustine, Bishop of Hippo in Northern Africa, made rules for the members of his order.

During this time an image was carved of the Blessed Virgin Mary whom Augustine regarded as their role model in loving God and loving their neighbors.

Thus the name Our Lady of Regla, or rule, became associated with the Augustinians.

When St. Augustine died and the Vandals invaded Africa, the monks fled to Spain and took the statue of Our Lady with them.

Following the invasion of the Saracens, the statue was hidden by the monks.

Centuries later, an Augustinian monk had a vision of Mary who told him to go to the sea of Cadiz and look for a cave.

Falling asleep under a fig tree, the monk had a vision that told him to dig beneath the tree to find the statue of Our Lady of Regla.

The monk dug until he came to a huge rock which he had to get the people of the town to help him move.

Beneath the rock was a cave and inside they found a box beside a burning lamp.

Our Lady of Regla, the statue St. Augustine had carved, was safely inside the box.

The location is now called Humilladero, and a church was built on that spot which houses the statue of Our Lady.

When the Augustinians founded the parish of Opon (now Lapu-Lapu), a large picture of Our Lady of Regla was put on the altar and she was made their patroness. Many miracles have been attributed to Our Lady.

Feast Day: November 21
Patron Saint: The Rule of Saint Augustine, Cebu

Our Lady of Altagracia

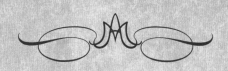

Most Holy Virgin of Altagracia,
from the bottom of our hearts, we thank you
for the continuous blessings you pour down on us. From
your hands and from your maternal heart
we receive, each day, the sustenance given to us
by our Heavenly Father. You are our defender
when we are in danger, our aid when we are in need
and our hope in the sacrifices proper
of our Christian life.
Through your Immaculate Heart
we want to sing a song of thanksgiving to God
for all the blessings he has given us.
We promise you, O Mother, gratitude and fidelity.
You will reign forever in our homes and our town
where we will venerate you as our Lady and Mother
by growing in all your virtues.
Make us worthy of being called your daughters
so that serving God and you on this world,
we will obtain the highest grace you bring to us:
a holy death that will open to us the gates of Heaven.
Amen.

Our Lady of Altagracia
History and Devotion

Around 1502, Alfonso and Antonio Trejo brought a portrait of the Blessed Virgin Mother from Spain to the island of Santa Domingo.

Upon moving to the city of Higuey, they donated the image to the parish church. The first shrine was built in 1572. The story is told that the devout daughter of a rich merchant asked her father to bring her a picture of Our Lady of Altagracia when he returned from his travels to Santa Domingo. Everyone he asked told him that they had never heard of that title of Mary.

He stopped in Higuey to stay overnight with a friend before returning home. Sitting outside at dinner, the merchant explained to his friend his bad fortune in search of the gift for his daughter. An old man passing by the table, reached in his knapsack and handed the merchant a rolled up painting, telling him that it was the image for his daughter.

The friend gave the old man a place to stay for the night but the next day, he was nowhere to be found. After receiving her gift, the daughter put the portrait on the mantle but it repeatedly disappeared only to be found outside the house.

The merchant finally returned Our Lady to the church.

The image portrays Mary watching over the Baby Jesus, which many local people believe symbolizes Our Lady watching over the island and the growth of Christianity.

The portrait was almost unrecognizable due to candle smoke and hand rubbing and was restored in Spain in 1978. In 1971, the Basilica to Our Lady was consecrated.

Feast Day: January 21
Patron Saint of: Dominican Republic

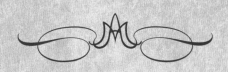

Our Lady of the Assumption

Mary,
God's Son became your Son and
you became both our Mother
and our Queen.
From your heavenly throne,
intercede for your subjects who are daily
confronted with life's trials.
Help us to find comfort in our
recourse to you and bring us closer
to your Divine Son whose glory and
honor we proclaim forever.
Amen.

Our Lady Queen
of the Apostles

Immaculate Mother of God, Queen of the Apostles,
we know that God's commandment of love
and our vocation to follow Jesus Christ
impels us to cooperate in the mission of the Church.
Realizing our own weakness,
we entrust the renewal of our personal lives
and our apostolate to your intercession.
We are confident that through God's mercy
and the infinite merits of Jesus Christ, you,
who are our Mother, will obtain the strength of the Holy Spirit
as you obtained it for the community of the apostles
gathered in the upper room.
Therefore, relying on your maternal intercession,
we resolve from this moment to devote our talents,
learning, material resources, our health, sickness and trials,
and every gift of nature and grace,
for the greater glory of God and the salvation of all.
We wish to carry on those activities
which especially promote the catholic apostolate
for the revival of faith and love of the people of God
and so bring all men and women into the faith of Jesus Christ.
And if a time should come
when we have nothing more to offer serviceable to this end,
we will never cease to pray that there will be one fold
and one shepherd Jesus Christ.
In this way, we hope to enjoy the results
of the apostolate of Jesus Christ for all eternity.
Amen.

CONGREGAVIT NOS IN UNUM CHRISTI AMOR

Our Lady the
Most Blessed Sacrament

Virgin Immaculate,
perfect lover of Our Lord in the Blessed Sacrament,
we ask you to obtain for us
the graces we need to become true adorers
of our Eucharistic God.
Grant us, we beg of you,
to know Him better,
to love Him more,
and to center our lives around the Eucharist,
that is, to make our whole life
a constant prayer of adoration,
thanksgiving, reparation,
and petition to Our Lord in the Blessed Sacrament.

Amen.

V. Pray for us, O Virgin Immaculate,
our Lady of the Most Blessed Sacrament
R. That the Eucharistic Kingdom of Jesus Christ
may come among us!

Prayer

O Lady of Mental Peace,
Mother of Tranquility and
Mother of Hope,
look upon me in this time
of my weakness and unrest.
Teach my searching heart to know that
God's Love for me is unchanging and
unchangeable; and, that true human
love can only begin
and grow by touching His Love.
Let your gentle Peace - which this world
cannot give - be always with me.
And, help me to bring this same peace
into the lives of others.
Our Lady of Mental Peace,
Pray for me!

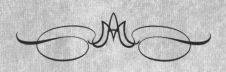

The Hail Mary

Hail Mary,
full of grace,
the Lord is with thee;
blessed art thou amongst women,
and blessed is the fruit of
thy womb, Jesus.
Holy Mary,
Mother of God,
pray for us sinners, now and at
the hour of our death.
Amen.

Magnificat

My soul does magnify the Lord
And my spirit has rejoiced in God my Savior.
Because He had regarded
the lowliness of His Servant.
For, behold from henceforth
all generations shall call me blessed.
For He that is mighty had done great things to me,
and holy is His Name.
And His mercy is from generation unto generation,
to them that fear Him.
He had showed might with His arm.
He had scattered the proud
in the conceit of their heart.
He had put down the mighty from their seat,
and had exalted the lowly.
He had filled the hungry with good things;
and the rich He had sent away empty.
He had received Israel His servant,
being mindful of His mercy.
As He spoke to our fathers,
to Abraham and to his seed forever.

The Memorare of St. Bernard

*Remember, O most gracious
Virgin Mary, that never was
it known that any one who fled
to thy protection, implored thy help,
and sought thy intercession,
was left unaided.
Inspired with this
confidence, I fly unto thee,
O Virgin of virgins, my Mother,
to thee I come, before thee
I kneel sinful and sorrowful.
O Mother of the Word Incarnate!
Despise not my petitions,
but, in thy mercy, hear and
answer me.
Amen.*

"To Our Lady"

Lovely Lady dressed in Blue,
Teach me how to pray!
God was just your little Boy,
Tell me what to say!
Did you lift Him up, sometimes,
Gently, on your knee?
Did you sing to Him the way
Mother does to me?
Did you hold His hand at night?
Did you ever try
Telling stories of the world?
O! And did He cry?
Do you really think He cares
If I tell Him things,
Little things that happen?
And do the Angels' wings
Make a noise? And can He hear
Me if I speak low?
Does He understand me now?
Tell me, for you know
Lovely Lady dressed in blue,
Teach me how to pray!
God was just your little Boy,
And you know the way.

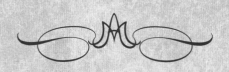

Prayer of St. Aloysius to the Blessed Mother

O holy Mary, my Mistress, into thy blessed
trust and special keeping, into the bosom
of thy tender mercy, this day, every day of
my life and at the hour of my death,
I commend my soul and body;
to thee I entrust all my hopes and
consolations, all my trials and miseries,
my life and the end of my life,
that through thy most holy intercession
and thy merits, all my actions may be
ordered and disposed according to thy
will and that of thy divine Son.
Amen.

Prayer to the Immaculate Heart of Mary
Novena Prayer

O MOST BLESSED MOTHER,
heart of love, heart of mercy,
ever listening, caring, consoling,
hear our prayer.
As your children, we implore your
intercession with Jesus your Son.
Receive with understanding and
compassion the petitions we place
before you today, especially
(special intention).
We are comforted in knowing your
heart is ever open to those
who ask for your prayer.
We trust to your gentle care and intercession,
those whom we love
and who are sick or lonely or hurting.
Help all of us, Holy Mother to bear
our burdens in this life until we
may share eternal life and peace
with God forever.
Amen.

An Offering to Mary

Here are my prayers, Mary
You do the rest
Where they are needed
You will know best.
Don't bother saving
A merit or two
Use them all, Mary,
I give them to you.
It's the only way, Mary,
That I can see.
For repaying my thanks
For the grace you gave me.
I give them to you
Without any strings,
Pass them to Jesus
As your offerings,
So take my prayers, Mary,
Add all that I do,
With my heart in the Center,

I give them to you.

O Mary Conceived Without Sin
Pray for us Who have
Recourse to Thee.

Ave, Regina Caelorum

Hail, O Queen of Heaven enthroned!
Hail, by angels Mistress owned
Root of Jesus,
Gate of morn,
Whence the world's true
Light was born.
Glorious Virgin, joy to thee,
Loveliest whom
in Heaven they see:
Fairest thou where
all are fair,
Plead with Christ
our sins to spare.

(Indulgence, 5 years; plenary, under usual
conditions, for month's recitation).

Prayer to the Immaculate Virgin

O Mary Ever Virgin most pure and Immaculate Daughter of the Eternal Father, Mother of the Eternal Son, Spouse of the Holy Ghost, august and living Temple of the Most Blessed Trinity, lily of purity and mirror without spot, obtain for me, O dear Mother, from thy good Jesus and mine, purity of soul and body, and beg of Him to make this virtue flourish more and more in all classes of the faithful.

Response: In thy conception, O Virgin Mary, thou wast immaculate. Pray for us to the Father, whose Son, Jesus Christ, conceived of The Holy Ghost thou didst bring forth. (300 days, each time S.P. April 24, 1932) Response: To thee, O Virgin Mother, never defiled by the slightest stain of original or actual sin, I commend and entrust the purity of my heart. Amen.

149

Mary

When you follow her,
You will not go astray;
When you pray to her,
You will not despair;
When you think of her,
You will not err;
When she holds you up,
You will not fail;
When she protects you,
You will not fear;
When she leads you,
You will not be fatigued;
When she favors you,
You will arrive safely.
She keeps her Son
from striking us;
She keeps the devil
from hurting us;
She keeps our virtues
from escaping us;
She keeps our merits
from being destroyed;
She keeps our graces
from being lost.
(St. Bernard)

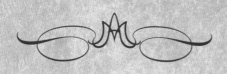

Invocations to Mary

May the Virgin Mary together
with her loving child bless us.
Pray for us,
O Holy Mother of God,
That we may be made worthy
of the promises of Christ.
Blessed be the Holy
and Immaculate
Conception of the
Blessed Virgin Mary,
Mother of God.
Holy Mother of God, Mary ever
Virgin intercede for us.
Amen.

My Queen My Mother

My Queen my Mother,
I give myself entirely
to thee, and to show
my devotion to thee,
I consecrate to you this
day my eyes, my ears,
my mouth, my heart,
my whole body without reserve.
Wherefore good Mother,
as I am thine own,
keep me and guard me
as your property
and possession.

Mater Amabilis

Prayer to Our Lady

May we be assisted,
we beseech Thee,
O Lord,
by the worshipful intercession
of Thy glorious Mother,
the ever-Virgin Mary;
that we who have been enriched
by her perpetual blessings,
may be delivered from all dangers,
and through her loving kindness
made to be of one heart and mind;
who livest and reignest world
without end.
Amen.

(Indulgence, 3 years; plenary, under usual
conditions, for month's recitation).
(Raccolta, No. 347)

Prayer to the Mother of God

It is truly right
to bless you,
O God-bearing One,
As the ever-Blessed
and most-pure
Mother of our God.
More honorable than
the cherubim and by
far more glorious
than the seraphim;
Who without corruption
gave birth to
God the Word,
O true
Mother of God
We magnify you.

The Golden Hail Mary

One fervent Hail Mary with love
and thought said
Is better than volumes of prayers poorly read,
If time and one's duties prevent a long prayer,
Just say one Hail Mary with fervor and care.
The "Golden Hail Mary"
which from the heart springs
The greatest of blessings from Mary it brings;
And we never will know till
before Mary's throne
How that daily Hail Mary
brought us to her home
If we dwell on the words,
"Mary, Mother of God,"
Do we not honor Jesus, her Son and her Lord?
And - "Pray for us now
and at the hour of our death" -
That moment when spiritual foes will be met.
Ah! that is the moment we'll surely need aid;
And to Mary we'll turn, that sweet,
lowly hand-maid.
Be sure she will help you if truly you say
One single Hail Mary - just one every day.
Amen.

THE ROSARY OF THE BLESSED VIRGIN MARY

The Rosary of the Virgin Mary, which gradually took form in the second century under the guidance of the Holy Spirit, is a prayer loved by countless Saints and encouraged by the Magisterium. Simple yet profound, it still remains, at the dawn of this third millenium, a prayer of great significance, destined to bring forth a harvest of holiness...

...With the Rosary, the Christian people sit at the school of Mary and are led to contemplate the beauty of the face of Christ and to experience the depths of His love. Through the Rosary the faithful receive abundant graces, as though from the very hands of the Mother of the Redeemer...

... Consequently, for the Rosary to become more fully a "summary of the Gospel", it is fitting to add, following reflection on the Incarnation and the hidden life of Christ (the joyful mysteries) and before focusing on the sufferings of His Passion (the sorrowful mysteries) and the triumph of His Resurrection (the glorious mysteries), a meditation on certain particularly significant moments in His public ministry (the mysteries of light). This addition of these new mysteries, without prejudice to any essential aspect of the prayer's traditional format, is meant to give it fresh life and to enkindle renewed interest in the Rosary's place within Christian spirituality as a true doorway to the depths of the Heart of Christ, ocean of joy and of light, of suffering and of glory.

PRAYERS OF THE ROSARY

The Sign of the Cross

In the name of the father, † and of the Son, and of the Holy Spirit.Amen.

The Apostles' Creed

I believe in God, the Father almighty, Creator of heaven and earth. I believe in Jesus Christ, His only Son, our Lord. He was conceived by the power of the Holy Spirit and born of the Virgin Mary. He suffered under Pontius Pilate, was crucified, died, and was buried. He descended to the dead. On the third day he rose again. He ascended into heaven and is seated at the right hand of the Father. He will come again to judge the living and the dead. I believe in the Holy Spirit, the holy catholic Church, the communion of saints, the forgiveness of sins, the resurrection of the body, and the life everlasting. Amen.

The Our Father

Our father who art in heaven, hallowed be Thy name; Thy kingdom come, Thy will be done on earth as it is in heaven. Give us this day our daily bread; and forgive us our trespasses as we forgive those who trespass against us. And lead us not into temptation; but deliver us from evil. Amen.

The Hail Mary

Hail Mary, full of grace, The Lord is with thee. Blessed art thou amongst women and blessed is the fruit of thy womb, Jesus. Holy Mary, Mother of God, pray for us sinners, now and at the hour of our death. Amen.

Glory Be to the Father

Glory be to the father, and to the Son, and to the Holy Spirit; as it was in the beginning, is now, and ever shall be, world without end. Amen.

The Fatima Prayer

O my Jesus, forgive us our sins, save us from the fires of hell. Lead all souls to heaven, especially those most in need of Thy mercy.

Hail, Holy Queen

Hail, holy Queen, Mother of Mercy! Our life, our sweetness, and our hope! To thee do we cry, poor banished children of Eve, to thee do we send up our sighs, mourning and weeping in this valley of tears. Turn then, most gracious advocate, thine eyes of mercy towards us; and after this, our exile show unto us the blessed fruit of thy womb, Jesus, O clement, O loving, O sweet Virgin Mary. Pray for us, O Holy Mother of God, that we may be made worthy of the promises of Christ.

V. Pray for us, O holy Mother of God.
R. That we may be made worthy
of the promises of Christ.

Let Us Pray

O God, whose only begotten Son, by His life, death, and resurrection has purchased for us the rewards of eternal life, grant, we beseech Thee, that meditating upon these mysteries of the Holy Rosary of the Blessed Virgin Mary, we may imitate what they contain, and obtain what they promise, through the same Christ our Lord. Amen.

HOW TO PRAY THE ROSARY

The Rosary is a form of vocal and mental prayer on the Mysteries of our Redemption.

The mysteries consist of 4 groups pictured on the following pages.

6. *Meditate on 3rd Mystery, saying the "Our Father", Ten "Hail Mary's" and "Glory Be".*

7. *Meditate on 4th Mystery, saying the "Our Father", Ten "Hail Mary's" and "Glory Be".*

5. *Meditate on 2nd Mystery, saying the "Our Father", Ten "Hail Mary's" and "Glory Be".*

8. *Meditate on 5th Mystery, saying the "Our Father", Ten "Hail Mary's" and "Glory Be".*

4. *Meditate on 1st Mystery, saying the "Our Father", Ten "Hail Mary's" and "Glory Be".*

9. *Concluding prayers, "Hail Holy Queen" and let us pray: "O God, Whose only begotten Son, etc."*

3. *Say three "Hail Mary's" and the "Glory Be".*

2. *Say the "Our Father".*

1. *Make the Sign of the Cross, Say the Apostles' Creed.*

Joyful Mysteries
To be said on Mondays and on Saturdays

The first five decades, the "joyful mysteries", are marked by the joy radiating from the event of the Incarnation...

... To meditate upon the "joyful" mysteries, then, is to enter into the ultimate causes and the deepest meaning of Christian joy.

It is to focus on the realism of the mystery of the Incarnation and on the obscure foreshadowing of the mystery of the saving Passion. Mary leads us to discover the secret of Christian joy, reminding us that Christianity is, first and foremost, evangelion, "good news", which has as its heart and its whole content the person of Jesus Christ, the Word made flesh, the one Saviour of the world.

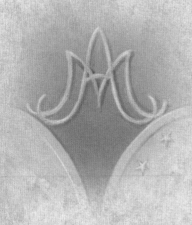

1ˢᵗ Joyful Mystery
The Annunciation
The Angel Gabriel tells Mary that she is to be the Mother of God.

5ᵗʰ Joyful Mystery
The Finding in the Temple
Jesus is lost for three days, and the Blessed Mother finds Him in the Temple.

2ⁿᵈ Joyful Mystery
The Visitation
The Blessed Virgin pays a visit to her cousin Elizabeth.

3ʳᵈ Joyful Mystery
The Nativity
The Infant Jesus is born in a stable at Bethlehem.

4ᵗʰ Joyful Mystery
The Presentation
The Blessed Virgin presents the Child Jesus to Simeon in the Temple.

1st JOYFUL MYSTERY
ANNUNCIATION

And coming in, he said to her,
"Greetings, favored one! The Lord is with you."
"And behold, you will conceive in your womb
and bear a son, and you shall name Him Jesus".
(Luke 1,28-31)

2ⁿᵈ JOYFUL MYSTERY
VISITATION

When Elizabeth heard Mary's greeting,
the baby leaped in her womb;
and Elizabeth was filled with the Holy Spirit.
And she cried out with a loud voice and said,
"Blessed are you among women,
and blessed is the fruit of your womb!"
(Luke 1,41-42)

3ʳᵈ JOYFUL MYSTERY
BIRTH OF JESUS

And she gave birth to her firstborn son;
and she wrapped Him in cloths,
and laid Him in a manger,
because there was no room for them in the inn.
(Luke 2,7)

4th Joyful Mystery
Presentation in the Temple

And when the days for their purification according to the law of Moses were completed, they brought Him up to Jerusalem to present Him to the Lord as it is written in the Law of the Lord, "every firstborn male that opens the womb shall be called holy to the Lord".
(Luke 2,22-23)

5th JOYFUL MYSTERY
FINDING THE CHILD JESUS

And He said to them,
"Why is it that you were looking for Me?
Did you not know that I had to be in My Father's house?"
And He went down with them and came to Nazareth,
and He continued in subjection to them;
and His mother treasured all these things in her heart.
(Luke 2,49-51)

MYSTERIES OF LIGHT

To be said on Thursdays

Moving on from the infancy and the hidden life in Nazareth to the public life of Jesus, our contemplation brings us to those mysteries which may be called in a special way "mysteries of light". Certainly the whole mystery of Christ is a mystery of light. He is the "light of the world" (Jn 8:12). Yet this truth emerges in a special way during the years of His public life, when He proclaims the Gospel of the Kingdom. In proposing to the Christian community five significant moments – "luminous" mysteries – during this phase of Christ's life, I think that the following can be fittingly singled out: (1) His Baptism in the Jordan, (2) His self-manifestation at the wedding of Cana, (3) His proclamation of the Kingdom of God, with His call to conversion, (4) His Transfiguration, and finally, (5) His institution of the Eucharist, as the sacramental expression of the Paschal Mystery...

... In these mysteries, apart from the miracle at Cana, the presence of Mary remains in the background. The Gospels make only the briefest reference to her occasional presence at one moment or other during the preaching of Jesus (cf. Mk 3:31-5; Jn 2:12), and they give no indication that she was present at the Last Supper and the institution of the Eucharist. Yet the role she assumed at Cana in some way accompanies Christ throughout His ministry. The revelation made directly by the Father at the Baptism in the Jordan and echoed by John the Baptist is placed upon Mary's lips at Cana, and it becomes the great maternal counsel which Mary addresses to the Church of every age: "Do whatever He tells you" (Jn 2:5). This counsel is a fitting introduction to the words and signs of Christ's public ministry and it forms the Marian foundation of all the "mysteries of light".

**1ˢᵗ Mystery of Light
The Baptism
of Jesus**
*Jesus is baptized in
the Jordan river by
John the Baptist.*

**5ᵗʰ Mystery of Light
The Institution
of Holy Eucharist**
*At supper with His apostles
before He dies, Jesus gives
himself to them
in bread and wine.*

**2ⁿᵈ Mystery of Light
The Wedding at Cana**
*Jesus attends a wedding at
Cana in Galilee, where he
turns water into wine.*

**4ᵗʰ Mystery of Light
The Transfiguration**
*Jesus leads His apostles up
a high mountain, where
they see Him shining
in glorious light.*

**3ʳᵈ Mystery of Light
The Proclamation of the
Kingdom of God**
*Jesus goes through the
towns and cities
of his own country
proclaiming God's
Kingdom and
helping the poor.*

1ˢᵗ MYSTERY OF LIGHT
CHRIST'S BAPTISM IN THE JORDAN

In those days Jesus came from Nazareth in Galilee and was baptized by John in the Jordan. Immediately coming up out of the water, He saw the heavens opening, and the Spirit like a dove descending upon Him; and a voice came out of the heavens: "You are My beloved Son, in You I am well-pleased." (Mark 1,9-10)

2nd MYSTERY OF LIGHT
WEDDING AT CANA

On the third day there was a wedding in Cana of Galilee, and the mother of Jesus was there; and both Jesus and His disciples were invited to the wedding. When the wine ran out, the mother of Jesus said to Him, "They have no wine." And Jesus said to her, "Woman, what does that have to do with us? My hour has not yet come." His mother said to the servants, "Whatever He says to you, do it."... and manifested His glory, and His disciples believed in Him. (John. 2,1-5)

3rd MYSTERY OF LIGHT
PROCLAMATION OF THE KINGDOM

Jesus was going throughout all Galilee, teaching in their synagogues and proclaiming the gospel of the kingdom, and healing every kind of disease and every kind of sickness among the people.
... Large crowds followed Him from Galilee and the Decapolis and Jerusalem and Judea and from beyond the Jordan. (Matt. 4,23,25)

4th MYSTERY OF LIGHT
TRANSFIGURATION

Six days later Jesus took with Him Peter and James and John his brother, and led them up on a high mountain by themselves. And He was transfigured before them; and His face shone like the sun, and His garments became as white as light.
And behold, Moses and Elijah appeared to them, talking with Him. (Matt. 17,1-3)

5th MYSTERY OF LIGHT
INSTITUTION OF THE EUCHARIST

*When the hour had come, He reclined at the table,
and the apostles with Him. And He said to them,
"I have earnestly desired to eat this Passover
with you before I suffer; for
I say to you, I shall never again eat it until it is fulfilled
in the kingdom of God." (Luke 22,14-16)*

SORROWFUL MYSTERIES

To be said on Tuesdays and on Fridays

The Gospels give great prominence to the sorrowful mysteries of Christ. From the beginning, Christian piety, especially during the Lenten devotion of the Way of the Cross, has focused on the individual moments of the Passion, realizing that here is found the culmination of the revelation of God's love and the source of our salvation. The Rosary selects certain moments from the Passion, inviting the faithful to contemplate them in their hearts and to relive them. The sequence of meditations begins with Gethsemane, where Christ experiences a moment of great anguish before the will of the Father, against which the weakness of the flesh would be tempted to rebel. There, Jesus encounters all the temptations and confronts all the sins of humanity, in order to say to the Father: "Not my will but yours be done" (Lk 22:42 and parallels). This "Yes" of Christ reverses the "No" of our first parents in the Garden of Eden. And the cost of this faithfulness to the Father's will is made clear in the following mysteries; by His scourging, His crowning with thorns, His carrying the Cross and His death on the Cross, the Lord is cast into the most abject suffering: Ecce homo!

This abject suffering reveals not only the love of God but also the meaning of man himself.

Ecce homo: the meaning, origin and fulfillment of man is to be found in Christ, the God who humbles Himself out of love "even unto death, death on a cross" (Phil 2:8). The sorrowful mysteries help the believer to relive the death of Jesus, to stand at the foot of the Cross beside Mary, to enter with her into the depths of God's love for man and to experience all its life-giving power.

1ˢᵗ Sorrowful Mystery
The Agony in the Garden
*Jesus prays in
the Garden of
Olives and drops
of blood break
through His skin.*

5ᵗʰ Sorrowful Mystery
The Crucifixion
*Jesus is nailed to the cross,
and dies for our sins.*

2ⁿᵈ Sorrowful Mystery
The Scourging at the Pillar
*Jesus is tied to a pillar
and cruelly beaten
with whips.*

4ᵗʰ Sorrowful Mystery
**The Carrying
of the Cross**
*Jesus is made to carry
His cross
to Calvary.*

3ʳᵈ Sorrowful Mystery
The Crowning with Thorns
*A crown of thorns is
placed upon Jesus' head.*

1ˢᵗ Sorrowful Mystery
Agony in the Garden

And being in agony He was praying very fervently;
and His sweat became like drops of blood,
falling down upon the ground.
(Luke 22,44)

2nd SORROWFUL MYSTERY
SCOURGING AT THE PILLAR

Wishing to satisfy the crowd, Pilate released Barabbas
for them, and after having Jesus scourged,
he handed Him over to be crucified.
(Mark 15,15)

3rd SORROWFUL MYSTERY
CROWNING WITH THORNS

*And after twisting together a crown of thorns,
they put it on His head, and a reed in His right hand;
and they knelt down before Him and mocked Him,
saying, "Hail, King of the Jews!"
They spat on Him, and took the reed and began
to beat Him on the head. (Matt. 27,29-30)*

4th Sorrowful Mystery
Carrying of the Cross

So he then handed Him over to them to be crucified.
They took Jesus, therefore, and He went out, bearing
His own cross, to the place called the Place of a Skull,
which is called in Hebrew, Golgotha.
(John 19,16-17)

5th Sorrowful Mystery
Crucifixion

Therefore when Jesus had received the sour wine,
He said, "It is finished!"
And He bowed His head and gave up His spirit.
(John 19,30)

GLORIOUS MYSTERIES

To be said on Wednesdays and on Sundays

"The contemplation of Christ's face cannot stop at the image of the Crucified One. He is the Risen One!" The Rosary has always expressed this knowledge born of faith and invited the believer to pass beyond the darkness of the Passion in order to gaze upon Christ's glory in the Resurrection and Ascension. Contemplating the Risen One, Christians rediscover the reasons for their own faith (cf. 1Cor 15:14) and relive the joy not only of those to whom Christ appeared – the Apostles, Mary Magdalene and the disciples on the road to Emmaus – but also the joy of Mary, who must have had an equally intense experience of the new life of her glorified Son. In the Ascension, Christ was raised in glory to the right hand of the Father, while Mary herself would be raised to that same glory in the Assumption, enjoying beforehand, by a unique privilege, the destiny reserved for all the just at the resurrection of the dead. Crowned in glory – as she appears in the last glorious mystery – Mary shines forth as Queen of the Angels and Saints, the anticipation and the supreme realization of the eschatological state of the Church. At the center of this unfolding sequence of the glory of the Son and the Mother, the Rosary sets before us the third glorious mystery, Pentecost, which reveals the face of the Church as a family gathered together with Mary, enlivened by the powerful outpouring of the Spirit and ready for the mission of evangelization. The contemplation of this scene, like that of the other glorious mysteries, ought to lead the faithful to an ever greater appreciation of their new life in Christ, lived in the heart of the Church, a life of which the scene of Pentecost itself is the great "icon"...

1ˢᵗ Glorious Mystery
The Resurrection
*Jesus rises from
the dead, three
days after His
death.*

5ᵗʰ Glorious Mystery
The Coronation
*The Blessed Virgin
is crowned Queen
of Heaven and Earth
by Jesus, her Son.*

2ⁿᵈ Glorious Mystery
The Ascension
*Forty days after His death,
Jesus Ascends into Heaven.*

4ᵗʰ Glorious Mystery
The Assumption
*The Blessed Virgin dies and
is Assumed into Heaven.*

3ʳᵈ Glorious Mystery
**The Descent
of the Holy Spirit**
*Ten days after
the Ascension,
the Holy Spirit comes to
the Apostles and
the Blessed Mother
in the form of flames.*

189

1ˢᵗ GLORIOUS MYSTERY
RESURRECTION

The angel said to the women, "Do not be afraid;
for I know that you are looking for Jesus who has been
crucified." He is not here, for He has risen,
just as He said.
(Matt. 28,5-6)

2nd GLORIOUS MYSTERY
ASCENSION INTO HEAVEN

So then, when the Lord Jesus had spoken to them,
He was received up into heaven and sat down
at the right hand of God.
(Mark 16-19)

3ʳᵈ GLORIOUS MYSTERY
DESCENT OF THE HOLY SPIRIT

And there appeared to them tongues of fire distributing
themselves, and they rested on each one of them.
And they were all filled with the Holy Spirit
and began to speak with other tongues,
as the Spirit was giving them utterance.
(Acts. 2,3-4)

4th Glorious Mystery
Assumption

*For behold, from this time
on all generations will count me blessed.
"For the Mighty One has done great things for me;
And holy is His name."
(Luke 1,48-49)*

5ᵗʰ GLORIOUS MYSTERY
CROWNING OF OUR BLESSED LADY

A great sign appeared in heaven: a woman clothed with the sun, and the moon under her feet, and on her head a crown of twelve stars.
(Revelation 12,1)

194

The 15 Promises of the Rosary

Given by the Blessed Virgin Mary to
St. Dominic and Blessed Alan de la Roche

1. Whoever shall faithfully serve me by praying the Rosary, shall receive signal graces.

2. I promise my special protection and the greatest graces to all those who shall recite the Rosary.

3. The Rosary shall be a powerful armor against hell, it will destroy vice, decrease sin, and defeat false teachings.

4. It will cause virtue and good works to flourish; it will obtain for souls the abundant mercy of God; it will withdraw the hearts of people from the love of the world and its vanities, and will lift them to the desire of eternal things. Oh, that souls would become holy by praying the Rosary.

5. The soul which recommends itself to me by praying the Rosary, shall not go to hell.

6. Whoever shall pray the Rosary devoutly, applying himself to the consideration of its

Sacred Mysteries shall never be conquered by disaster. God will not punish him in His justice; if he be good, he shall remain in the grace of God, and become worthy of eternal life.

7. Whoever shall have a true devotion for the Rosary shall not die without the Sacraments of the Church.

8. Those who are faithful to pray the Rosary shall have during their life and at their death the light of God and all His graces; at the moment of death they shall participate in the merits of the Saints in Paradise.

9. I shall deliver from Purgatory those who have been devoted to the Rosary.

10. The faithful children of the Rosary shall become great in Heaven.

11. You shall obtain all you ask of me by the recitation of the Rosary.

12. All those who spread the Holy Rosary shall be aided by me in their necessities.

13. I have obtained from my Divine Son that

all the advocates of the Rosary shall have for intercessors all the Angels and Saints in Heaven during their life and at the hour of death.

14. All who pray the Rosary are my children, and brothers and sisters of my only Son, Jesus Christ.

15. Devotion to my Rosary is a great sign that you are going to go to Heaven.

THE "54-day ROSARY NOVENA"

The "54-DAY Rosary Novena" is an uninterrupted series of Rosaries in honor of Our Lady, revealed to the incurably sick Fortuna Agrelli by Our Lady of Pompei at Naples in 1884.

On March 3rd of that year, after Fortuna and her relatives had begun a novena of Rosaries for a cure, Our Blessed Mother appeared to her saying; "Make three novenas and you will obtain your request."

Later, Our Blessed Lady said to her: "whoever wishes to receive favors from me should make three novenas of the prayers of the Rosary in petition and three novenas in thanksgiving."

The Devotion consists of the Rosary of petition said every day for twenty-seven days; then, regardless of whether or not you have received your request, immediately begin the Rosary of thanksgiving every day for twenty-seven days.

The Angelus

Traditionally, the Church invites us to pray the Angelus, in the morning, at noon, and in the evening, but especially at noon. It is a special prayer that reminds us of when Jesus became a Baby in Mary's womb. By praying this prayer, we honor Jesus and Mary. It is a good way to make our whole day a prayer.

V. The angel spoke God's message to Mary,
R. And she conceived of the Holy Spirit.
Hail Mary…

V. I am the lowly servant of the Lord,
R. Let it be done to me according to your word.
Hail Mary…

V. And the Word became flesh,
R. And lived among us.
Hail Mary…

V. Pray for us, holy Mother of God,
R. That we may become worthy of the promises of Christ.

Let us pray.

Lord, fill our hearts with Your grace: once, through the message of an angel, you revealed to us the incarnation of your Son; now, through his suffering and death, lead us to the glory of his resurrection. We ask this through Christ our Lord.

R. Amen.

REGINA CAELI (For Easter Time)
V. Queen of Heaven, rejoice! Alleluia.
R. For He whom you did merit to bear. Alleluia.
V. Has risen, as He said. Alleluia.
R. Pray for us to God. Alleluia.
V. Rejoice and be glad, O Virgin Mary, Alleluia.
R. For the Lord is truly risen. Alleluia.

Let us pray, O God, who gave joy to the world through the Resurrection of Your Son our Lord Jesus Christ, grant we beseech You that through the intercession of the Virgin Mary, His Mother, we may obtain the joys of everlasting life, through the same Christ our Lord.

R. Amen.

CONSECRATION TO JESUS CHRIST THROUGH MARY

(Adapted from St. Louis Mary de Montfort)

I,_____ a repentant sinner, renew in your hands the vows of my Baptism; I renounce forever Satan, his pomps and works; and I give myself entirely to Jesus Christ, promising to be more faithful to Him than I have ever been before. In the presence of all the heavenly court I choose you this day for my Mother.

I give to you my body and soul, my goods, both interior and exterior, and even the value of my good actions, past present, and future; for the greater glory of God in time and in eternity.
Amen.

TOTUS TUUS   **TOTALLY YOURS**

TO JESUS THROUGH MARY

Litany of the Blessed Virgin

Lord have mercy,	*Christ, have mercy*
Lord have mercy,	
God our Father in heaven,	*have mercy on us.*
God the Son, Redeemer of the world,	*have mercy on us.*
God the Holy Spirit,	*have mercy on us.*
Holy Trinity, one God,	*have mercy on us.*
Holy Mary,	*pray for us.*
Holy Mother of God,	*pray for us.*
Most honored of virgins,	*pray for us.*
Mother of Christ,	*pray for us.*
Mother of the Church,	*pray for us.*
Mother of divine grace,	*pray for us.*
Mother most pure,	*pray for us.*
Mother of chaste love,	*pray for us.*
Mother and virgin,	*pray for us.*
Sinless Mother,	*pray for us.*
Dearest of Mothers,	*pray for us.*
Model of motherhood,	*pray for us.*
Mother of good counsel,	*pray for us.*
Mother of our Creator,	*pray for us.*
Mother of our Savior,	*pray for us.*
Virgin most wise,	*pray for us.*
Virgin rightly praised,	*pray for us.*
Virgin rightly renowned,	*pray for us.*
Virgin most powerful,	*pray for us.*
Virgin gentle in mercy,	*pray for us.*
Faithful Virgin,	*pray for us.*
Mirror of justice,	*pray for us.*
Throne of wisdom,	*pray for us.*
Cause of our joy,	*pray for us.*
Shrine of the Spirit,	*pray for us.*
Glory of Israel,	*pray for us.*
Vessel of selfless devotion,	*pray for us.*
Mystical Rose,	*pray for us.*
Tower of David,	*pray for us.*

Tower of ivory,	*pray for us.*
House of gold,	*pray for us.*
Gate of heaven,	*pray for us.*
Morning Star,	*pray for us.*
Health of the sick,	*pray for us.*
Refuge of sinners,	*pray for us.*
Comfort of the troubled,	*pray for us.*
Help of Christians,	*pray for us.*
Queen of angels,	*pray for us.*
Queen of patriarchs and prophets,	*pray for us.*
Queen of apostles and martyrs,	*pray for us.*
Queen of confessors and virgins,	*pray for us.*
Queen of all saints,	*pray for us.*
Queen conceived without sin,	*pray for us.*
Queen assumed into heaven,	*pray for us.*
Queen of the rosary,	*pray for us.*
Queen of the family,	*pray for us.*
Queen of peace,	*pray for us.*

Lamb of God, You take away the sins of the world,	*have mercy on us.*
Lamb of God, You take away the sins of the world,	*have mercy on us.*
Lamb of God, You take away the sins of the world,	*have mercy on us.*

V. Pray for us, holy Mother of God.

R. That we may become worthy of the promises of Christ.

Let us pray.

Eternal God, let your people enjoy constant health in mind and body.

Through the intercession of the Virgin Mary free us from the sorrows of this life and lead us to happiness in the life to come. Grant this through Christ our Lord.

Amen.

The Prayers of Fatima

Say often when doing good deeds:

O Jesus, it is for Your love, for the conversion of sinners, and in reparation for the sins committed against the Immaculate Heart of Mary.

When visiting Jesus in the Blessed Sacrament, say: My God, I believe, I adore, I hope, and I love You. I ask pardon for those who do not believe, do not adore, do not hope, and do not love You.

Most Holy Trinity; Father, Son and Holy Spirit, I adore You profoundly, and I offer You the most precious Body, Blood, Soul, and Divinity of Jesus Christ present in all the tabernacles of the world in reparation for the outrages, sacrileges, and indifferences with which He is offended; and by the infinite merits of His Most Sacred Heart and of the Immaculate Heart of Mary I ask You for the conversion of poor sinners.

TO MARY

O Mary, my Queen, my Mother! I consecrate to you my eyes, my ears, my mouth, my heart, my entire self.

O loving Mother, because I am your own, keep me; defend me as your property and possession.

THE BROWN SCAPULAR

A special devotion to Mary is the Brown Scapular. She gave it to St. Simon Stock. We wear it around our neck to show our love for Mary and our trust in her protection. What a wonderful gift to receive, and begin wearing it on the day of our First Holy Communion.

Mary has promised that if we wear the Scapular with devotion and do our best to please God, then we will always have her motherly protection, and will not suffer the eternal fires of hell. When the Blessed Mother came to the three children of Fatima, she was holding the Brown Scapular in her hand. She shows us that she wants everyone to pray the Rosary every day and to wear the Brown Scapular.

St. Simon Stock
Pray for us

Our Lady of Mount Carmel
Pray for us

FIRST SATURDAY DEVOTION

The First Saturday Devotion to the Immaculate Heart of Mary was first mentioned by Our Lady of Fatima on July 13, 1917. After showing the three children a vision of hell she said, "You have seen hell where the souls of poor sinners go. To save them, God wishes to establish in the world devotion to my Immaculate Heart. If what I say to you is done, many souls will be saved and there will be peace... I shall come to ask for... the Communion of reparation on the first Saturdays..." Eight years later, on December 10, 1925, Mary and the Child Jesus appeared to Lucia, the sole surviving Fatima visionary, at a convent in Pontevedra, Spain. Our Lady rested her hand on Lucia's shoulder, revealing a heart encircled by thorns. The Child Jesus said: "Have compassion on the heart of your most holy Mother, covered with thorns with which ungrateful men pierce it at every moment, and there is no one to make an act of reparation..." Our Lady spoke next, saying: "Look, my daughter, at my heart, surrounded with thorns with which ungrateful men pierce it at every moment by their blasphemies and ingratitude. You at least try to console me and say that I promise to assist at the hour of death, with the graces necessary for salvation, all those who, *on the first Saturday of five consecutive months, shall*

confess, receive Holy Communion, recite five decades of the Rosary, and keep me company for fifteen minutes while meditating on fifteen mysteries of the Rosary, with the intention of making reparation to me."

SEVEN JOYS OF THE BLESSED VIRGIN MARY

1. The Annunciation of the Blessed Virgin Mary.
2. The Visitation of the Blessed Virgin Mary.
3. The Nativity of Our Lord & Adoration of the Magi.
4. The Presentation of Our Lord and Purification of the Blessed Virgin Mary.
5. The Finding of Our Lord in the Temple.
6. The Resurrection of Our Lord.
7. The Assumption of the Blessed Virgin Mary.

SEVEN SORROWS OF THE BLESSED VIRGIN MARY

1. The Prophecy of Simeon.
2. The Flight into Egypt.
3. The Loss of Our Lord in Jerusalem.
4. The Meeting of Our Lord on the Way to Calvary.
5. The Standing at the Foot of the Cross.
6. The Taking Down of Our Lord from the Cross.
7. The Burial of Our Lord.

THE THIRTY DAY
PRAYER TO MARY

Ever glorious and blessed Mary, Queen of Virgins, Mother of Mercy, hope and comfort of dejected and desolate souls, through the sword of sorrow which pierced your tender heart while your only Son, Christ Jesus, our Lord, suffered death and ignominy on the cross; through that filial tenderness and pure love He had for you, grieving at your grief, while from His cross He recommended you to the care and protection of His beloved disciple, Saint John, take pity, I beg you, on my poverty and necessities; have compassion on my anxieties and cares; assist and comfort me in all my infirmities and miseries, of what kind so ever.

You are the Mother of Mercies, the sweet comforter and only refuge of the needy and the orphan, of the desolate and afflicted.

Cast, therefore, an eye of pity on a miserable, forlorn child of Eve, and hear my prayer; for since, in just punishment of my sins, I find myself encompassed by a multitude of evils, and oppressed with much anguish of spirit, where can I fly for more secure shelter, O amiable Mother of my Lord and Savior, Jesus Christ, than under the wings of your maternal

protection? Attend, therefore, I beg you, with an ear of pity and compassion, to my humble and earnest request.

I ask it, through the bowels of mercy of your dear Son; through that love and condescension which He embraced your nature, when in compliance with the divine will, you gave your consent, and whom, after the expiration of nine months, you brought forth from the chaste enclosure your womb, to visit this world, and bless it with His presence.

I ask it, through that anguish of mind wherewith your beloved Son, our Dear Savior, was overwhelmed on Mount of Olives, when He besought His eternal Father to remove from Him, if possible, the bitter chalice of His future passion.

I ask it, through the threefold repetition of His prayers in the Garden, from where afterwards, with dolorous steps and mournful tears, you accompanied Him to the doleful theater of His death and sufferings.

I ask it, through the welts and sores of His virginal flesh, occasioned by the cords and whips wherewith He was bound and scourged, when stripped of His seamless garment, for which His executioners afterwards cast lots.

I ask it, through the scoffs and ignominies by

which He was insulted; the false accusations and unjust sentence by which He was condemned to death, and which He bore with heavenly patience.

I ask it, through His bitter tears and bloody sweat; His silence and resignation, His sadness and grief of heart.

I ask it, through the blood which trickled from His royal and Sacred Head, when struck with the scepter of a reed, and pierced with His crown of thorns.

I ask it, through the excruciating torments He suffered, when His hands and feet were fastened with gross nails to the tree of the cross.

I ask it, through His vehement thirst, and bitter potion of vinegar and gall.

I ask it, through His dereliction on the cross, when He exclaimed; "My God! My God! Why hast Thou forsaken me?"

I ask it, through His mercy extended to the good thief, and through His recommending His precious soul and spirit into the hands of His eternal Father before He expired, saying: "All is consummated".

I ask it, through the blood mixed with water, which issued from His Sacred Side when pierced with a lance and from where a flood of grace and mercy has flowed to us.

I ask it, through His immaculate life, bitter passion, and ignominious death on the cross, at which nature itself was thrown into convulsions, by the bursting of rocks, rending of the veil of the Temple, the earthquake, and darkness of the sun and moon.

I ask it, through His descent into hell, where He comforted the Saints of the old law with His presence, and led captivity home.

I ask it, through His glorious victory over death, when He arose again to life on the third day, and through the joy which His appearance for forty days after gave you, His blessed Mother, His Apostles, and the rest of His Disciples; when in your and their presence He miraculously ascended into Heaven.

I ask it, through the grace of the Holy Spirit, infused into the hearts of His Disciples; when He descended upon them in the form of fiery tongues; and by which they were inspired with zeal for the conversion of the world when they went forth to preach the Gospel.

I ask it, through the awful appearance of your Son, at the last dreadful day, when He shall come to judge the living and the dead, and the world by fire.

I ask it, through the compassion He bore thee in this life, and the ineffable joy you felt

at your assumption into Heaven, where you are eternally absorbed in the sweet contemplation of His divine perfections.

O glorious and ever blessed Virgin! Comfort the heart of your supplicant, by obtaining for me (here mention your request). And as I am persuaded my Divine Savior does honor you as His beloved Mother, to whom He refuses nothing, because you ask nothing contrary to His honor, so let me speedily experience the efficacy of your powerful intercession, according to the tenderness of your maternal affection, and His filial loving heart, Who mercifully grants the requests and complies with the desires of those that love and fear Him.

O most blessed Virgin, beside the object of my present petition, and whatever else I may stand in need of, obtain for me also from your dear Son, our Lord and our God, a lively faith, firm hope, perfect charity, true contrition of heart, unfeigned tears of compunction, sincere confession, suitable satisfaction, abstinence from sin, love of God and my neighbor, contempt of the world, patience to suffer affronts and ignominies, even, if necessary, an offensive death itself, for love of your Son, our Savior Jesus Christ.

Obtain likewise for me, O sacred Mother of

God, perseverance in good works, performance of good resolutions, mortification of self will, a pious conversation through life, and, at my last moments, strong and sincere repentance, accompanied by such a lively and attentive presence of mind, as may enable me to receive the last Sacrament of the church worthily, and die in your friendship and favor.

Lastly, obtain through your Son, I beg you, for the souls of my parents, brethren, relatives and benefactors, both living and dead, life everlasting, from the only Giver of every good and perfect gift, the Lord God Almighty: to Whom be all power now and forever. Amen.

CHRONOLOGICAL LIST OF
FEAST DAYS OF MARY

January 1: Solemnity of Mary
January 8: Our Lady of Prompt Succor
February 2: Presentation of the Lord
February 11: Our Lady of Lourdes
March 25: Annunciation
May 13: Our Lady of Fatima
May 31: Visitation
June 27: Our Mother of Perpetual Help
July 16: Our Lady of Mount Carmel
August 15: Assumption
August 22: Queenship of Mary
September 8: Birth of Mary
September 12: The Most Holy Name of Mary
September 15: Our Lady of Sorrows
September 24: Our Lady of Walsingham, England
October 7: Our Lady of the Rosary
October 8: Our Lady of Good Remedy
November 21: Presentation of the Blessed Virgin Mary
December 8: Immaculate Conception
December 12: Our Lady of Guadalupe

CONTENTS